1812–14

French Guardsman

VERSUS

Russian Jaeger

Laurence Spring

First published in Great Britain in 2013 by Osprey Publishing,
PO Box 883, Oxford OX1 9PL, UK
PO Box 3985, New York, NY 10185-3985, USA
E-mail: info@ospreypublishing.com

OSPREY PUBLISHING IS PART OF THE OSPREY GROUP

A CIP catalogue record for this book is available from the British
Library

Print ISBN: 978 1 78200 362 5
PDF ebook ISBN: 978 1 4728 0611 6
ePub ebook ISBN: 978 1 4728 0612 3

Index by Alan Thatcher
Typeset in Univers, Sabon and Adobe Garamond Pro
Maps by bounford.com
Artwork by Mark Stacey
Originated by PDQ Media, Bungay, UK
Printed in China through Asia Pacific Offset Ltd

13 14 15 16 17   10 9 8 7 6 5 4 3 2 1

Osprey Publishing is supporting the Woodland Trust, the UK's
leading woodland conservation charity, by funding the dedication
of trees.

www.ospreypublishing.com

Author's acknowledgements

I would like to thank the British Library, the Russian State
Library, the Bibliothèque Nationale, the Service historique de la
Défence and the Edinburgh University Library for their assistance
in writing this book. Thanks are due to Alexander Mikaberidze
(AM); Anne S.K. Brown Military Collection, Brown University
Library (ASKB); Neil Grant; the Royal Armouries and René
Chartrand (RC) for use of their images, which helped so vividly
to illustrate this work. Special mention should also go to Nick
Reynolds, the editor of the Combat series, and to Mark Stacey
for his excellent artwork plates.

Author's note

The life of the private soldier and the Russian Army of the
Napoleonic period have always fascinated me, so I have wanted
to write a book like this for a long time. It also gave me the
opportunity to research Napoleon's Grande Armée. By using not
only written accounts, but also archaeological evidence as well as
medical and pension records I hope I have produced a book
which does justice to the Napoleonic soldier.

Artist's note

Readers may care to note that the original paintings from which
the artwork plates in this book were prepared are available for
private sale. All reproduction copyright whatsoever is retained by
the Publishers. All enquiries should be addressed to:

mark@mrstacey.plus.com

The publishers regret that they can enter into no correspondence
upon this matter.

Editor's acknowledgements

The editor is indebted to Trevor Bounford and Denise Goodey
for their patience and expertise in drawing the maps for
this book.

Editor's note

For clarity, both French and Russian measurements current
in the period have been converted into metric in this book.
The following will help in converting between imperial and
metric measurements:
1 mile = 1.6km
1yd = 0.9m
1ft = 0.3m
1in = 2.54cm/25.4mm
1lb = 0.45kg

Comparative officer ranks

	Russian	French
colonel	*polkovnik*	*colonel*
lieutenant-colonel	*podpolkovnik*	*major*
major	*major*	*chef de bataillon*
captain	*kapitan*	*capitaine*
staff-captain	*shtabs-kapitan*	no equivalent
lieutenant	*poruchik*	*lieutenant*
2nd lieutenant	*podporuchik*	*sous-lieutenant*
cadet	*unker*	no equivalent
ensign	*praporshchik*	no equivalent
officer candidate	*portupei-praporshchik*	no equivalent

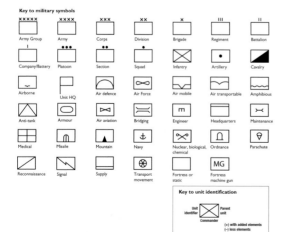

Key to military symbols

CONTENTS

Introduction

An unsigned portrait of Napoleon I (1769–1821), *c.* 1812. The French emperor's Imperial Guard would save his field army at Krasnyi and provide its principal striking force in the campaigns of 1813 and 1814. Devotion to the person of the emperor came under increasing pressure as the wars went against France after 1812, but remained a potent motivation for Napoleon's Guardsmen until the end. (RC)

In April 1814, Napoleon wanted to die. Paris had fallen to the Allies and so, believing there was no other option but suicide, the French emperor swallowed the poison he had worn around his neck since nearly being captured by the Russians during the retreat from Moscow two years earlier. In the event the poison failed, and the emperor was exiled to Elba, only to return in a last effort to wrest back his throne during the 'Hundred Days' in 1815.

It was a far cry from those days when the young Bonaparte had saved the French Revolution and was made First Consul and then emperor. Magnificent victories followed – Austerlitz, Jena and Auerstädt, Friedland and Wagram – which made Napoleon the master of Europe. In 1812 there had been an air of anticipation that Napoleon would once again be victorious, this time against Russia. In his memoirs, Sous-lieutenant Paul de Bourgoing of the 5th Tirailleurs recalled his feelings on the eve of the campaign:

> You can not imagine the enthusiasm with which the young men prepared for this distant expedition. I was nineteen at the time and we were so confident of success that, thinking of our ambition and chances of promotion, we regarded this campaign, with regret, as the time that the Emperor would have to try his luck in battle in order to conquer the world. (Quoted in Uffindell 2007: 77)

There was also excitement in Russia. Among those watching the Russian soldiers marching to the frontier was 13-year-old Alexander Pushkin, the future poet, who attended school near St Petersburg:

ALÉXANDRE PREMIER EMPEREUR DE TOUTES LES RUSSIES.

Tsar Alexander I (1777–1825), by Charles François Gabriel Levachez, *c.* 1813–14. Initially somewhat impressed by the French ruler, Alexander was by 1812 determined to crush Napoleon and was at the centre of the coalition effort to defeat France in 1812–14. (ASKB)

To begin with we saluted all the regiments of the Guard which marched through Tsarskoe-Selo. We were always there as soon as they came in sight, and we even went out to meet them during lessons. We accompanied them with a fervent prayer, we kissed our relations and friends, and grenadiers wearing heavy moustaches blessed us with a sign of the cross without leaving the ranks. How many tears we shed! (Quoted in Spring 2009: 18)

Many of Tsar Alexander's officers wanted their ruler to order an invasion of the Duchy of Warsaw, Napoleon's Polish satellite state, and then Germany, but in the end when war did come it would be a defensive campaign for the Russians. The Russians' initial retreat towards Moscow would be followed by their dogged pursuit of the Grande Armée to the borders of Russia's empire and beyond, and ultimately to the gates of Paris in the spring of 1814.

The regiments of Napoleon's Imperial Guard and Russia's Jaeger – light infantry – arm would be at the centre of these campaigns for supremacy in Europe. In 1809 Napoleon had increased the size of his Imperial Guard, dividing it into the Old, Middle and Young Guard, and would continue to raise new regiments for his Young Guard almost up to his abdication. For many years the men of the Imperial Guard were looked upon with resentment and envy by the rest of the French Army, since they were given preferential treatment. By the end of the 1814 campaign the regiments of the Young Guard were on paper an immense elite formation, but in reality the regiments were hastily trained, poorly equipped and so under-strength that they mustered little more than weak battalions, and battalions were just companies.

Of course any regiment on either side could act as skirmishers if required, but the benefits of open-order tactics were not lost on Tsar Alexander or his generals. During the French Revolutionary Wars and the early campaigns of the 19th century the Russian Jaeger were no match for their French counterparts, but by 1812 they had gained valuable experience in the art of light-infantry warfare and became the equals of the French, if not better. Seeing their usefulness, the Tsar converted musketeer regiments into Jaeger units, as well as raising new ones. Within the Russian Lifeguard, Alexander expanded the Jaeger battalion to regimental strength and raised the Finland Guards Regiment, which was designated, dressed and equipped as a light-infantry regiment. Unlike Napoleon, Alexander channelled virtually all his fresh manpower into existing regiments; this meant that the veterans were able to train the new recruits, and so the fighting capabilities of the regiments were preserved and enhanced.

Soldiers of the 41st Jaeger Regiment in May 1815, drawn by Johann Adam Klein and coloured by Georg Schäfer. This regiment served with the 12th Infantry Division alongside the 6th Jaeger Regiment; the light-blue shoulder-straps visible here indicate the junior Jaeger regiment of the Division. The grenadier company junior officer shown here wears grey overalls, gorget, unfringed epaulettes, waist-sash and knapsack, but retains an NCO's shako pompon quartered in white and mixed black and orange. The grenadier company NCO to his left wears a white-tipped plume and lace edging to his cuffs and collar; this edging should be gold, not white. (ASKB)

In the three battles examined here, which stretch over the last years of the Napoleonic Wars, the decline of the Young Guard and the rise of the Russian Jaeger arm are starkly exposed. I have chosen to focus on the battlefield performance of three of Napoleon's Voltigeur regiments – the 1st, 2nd and 14th – and that of the two Lifeguard Jaeger units, together with the 19th Jaeger Regiment, a unit that benefitted greatly from its extensive experience of warfare against the Ottomans and others before it joined the fight against Napoleon. Although Napoleon's *tirailleur* regiments also saw widespread combat against Alexander's forces, the sources consulted in the preparation of this book favoured the *voltigeurs*, and their experiences and performance are in any event likely to have been very similar to those of their *tirailleur* brethren. Similarly, the longevity and high profile of the two Jaeger regiments of Alexander's Lifeguard meant that it was possible to form a much more detailed picture of their combat performance than it would have been to do so for many of the 'Line' Jaeger regiments.

At Krasnyi, the rearguard actions of the 1st Voltigeurs and other Young Guard units demonstrated that the Grande Armée could still bite back. It is widely believed that on the Russian side only the cavalry and artillery were involved, but the Guards Jaeger Regiment played a key role in the defeat and destruction of the 1st Voltigeurs alongside the Reval Infantry Regiment and the Finland Guards Regiment, among others.

At Güldengossa – a hard-fought action, but just one of many in the titanic 'Battle of the Nations', as the epic clash at Leipzig in October 1813 was called – we explore the involvement of the 2nd Voltigeurs, a regiment that had recently been recalled from Spain and so had avoided the ravages of the Russian campaign, and the Finland Guards Regiment. Among those who took part in this action was Pamfil Nazarov, the only Russian infantryman known to have left an account of his military life during the Napoleonic Wars.

The third battle examined here, Craonne, was the bloodiest of the 1814 campaign until the battle of Paris. Here we witness the combat role of the ill-fated 14th Voltigeurs and the seasoned 19th Jaeger Regiment; the fates of these two very different units exemplify the differences in expertise, confidence and reputation that had opened up between the Young Guard and the Jaeger in the months since Napoleon's fateful decision to invade Russia.

A *Flanquer-grenadier* of the Imperial Guard, after Carle Vernet. Uniformed, like their colleagues in the Flanquers-chasseurs, in green with yellow piping rather than the blue worn by the bulk of the Young Guard infantry, the Flanquers-grenadiers were formed in 1813; unusually, they wore shako-cords, which were officially suppressed for the Tirailleurs and Voltigeurs in that year, and yellow lace edging on their gaiters. The single cross-belt, lack of sabre and lapels closed to the waist are characteristic of the appearance of the Young Guard after April 1813. (RC)

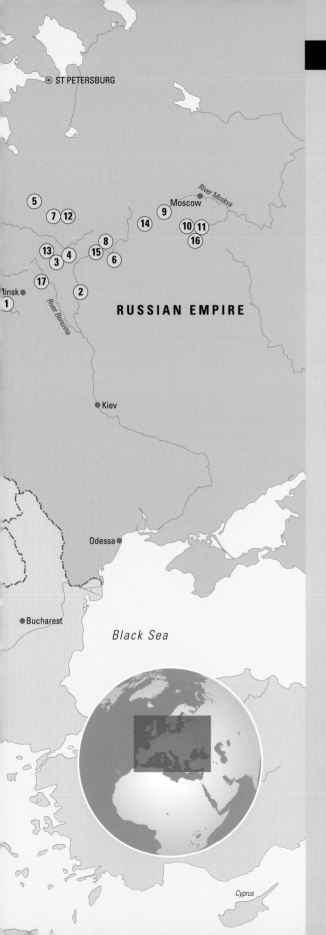

Battles involving French and Russian forces, 1812–14

1 Mir, 9–10 July 1812
2 Saltanovka, 23 July 1812
3 Ostrovna, 25 July 1812
4 Vitebsk, 26–27 July 1812
5 Klyastitsy, 28 July-1 August 1812
6 Smolensk, 16–18 August 1812
7 1st Polotsk, 17–18 August 1812
8 Valutino, 18 August 1812
9 Borodino, 7 September 1812
10 Tarutino, 18 October 1812
11 Maloyaroslavets, 24 October 1812
12 2nd Polotsk, 18–20 October 1812
13 Czasniki, 31 October 1812
14 Vyazma, 3 November 1812
15 Smoliani, 13–14 November 1812
16 Krasnyi, 15–18 November 1812
17 Berezina, 26–29 November 1812
18 Möckern, 5 April 1813
19 Weißenfels, 1 May 1813
20 Lützen, 2 May 1813
21 Bautzen, 20–21 May 1813
22 Haynau, 26 May 1813
23 Luckau, 6 June 1813
24 Großbeeren, 23 August 1813
25 Katzbach, 26 August 1813
26 Dresden, 26–27 August 1813
27 Hagelberg, 27 August 1813
28 Nollendorf, 29–30 August 1813
29 Kulm, 30 August 1813
30 Dennewitz, 6 September 1813
31 Wartenberg, 3 October 1813
32 Liebertwolkwitz, 14 October 1813
33 Leipzig, 16–19 October 1813
34 Hanau, 30–31 October 1813
35 Brienne, 29 January 1814
36 La Rothière, 1 February 1814
37 Champaubert, 10 February 1814
38 Montmirail, 11 February 1814
39 Château-Thierry, 12 February 1814
40 Vauchamps, 14 February 1814
41 Montereau, 18 February 1814
42 Bar-sur-Aube, 27 February 1814
43 Craonne, 7 March 1814
44 Laon, 9–10 March 1814
45 Reims, 13 March 1814
46 Arcis-sur-Aube, 20–21 March 1814
47 Fère-Champenoise, 25 March 1814
48 Saint-Dizier, 26 March 1814
49 Montmartre, 30 March 1814
50 Paris, 30–31 March 1814

The Opposing Sides

ORIGINS AND COMBAT ROLE

Russian

In Russian usage, the word 'Yeger' (originally a German term, anglicised here as 'Jaeger') was employed to indicate general-purpose light infantry, able to perform the standard infantry roles but also tasked with skirmishing – countering the enemy's extended-order infantry and harassing his close-order units, notably officers and artillery personnel, with individual, aimed fire. There

had been Jaeger corps in the Russian Army during the reign of Catherine II the Great (r. 1762–96), but it was under her son, Tsar Paul I (r. 1796–1801), that the Jaeger regiments took the form in which they fought the Napoleonic Wars. Under Tsar Alexander I (r. 1801–25), unlike the infantry and grenadier regiments, which had mostly geographical titles, each Jaeger regiment was known by a number. The 1st to 19th Jaeger regiments were established in 1797, while those up to the 32nd were raised in 1803–06. In 1810 14 'musketeer' (line infantry) regiments were converted into Jaeger regiments, while four more were raised the following year – making a total of 50 regiments on the eve of Napoleon's invasion, together fielding, in theory, more than 100,000 men. The Jaeger arm also included the Guards Jaeger Regiment and the Finland Guards Regiment, and a Jaeger company would serve in the Russo-German Legion, raised from prisoners taken by the Russians during the 1812 campaign. In April 1813 a further three regiments were established, bringing the total number to 55 (plus second-line wartime formations such as the regiment raised by Alexander's sister, the Grand Duchess Ekaterina Pavlovni, in 1812).

The general reorganization of the Russian Army that took place in the wake of defeat in 1805–07 centred on the establishment of French-style 'Divisions' rather than the previous 'Inspections'. Jaeger regiments were allocated to infantry Divisions in pairs, forming a third infantry brigade in each Division, alongside integral artillery units; these Divisions were then grouped in corps. Senior commanders like Kutuzov, Barclay de Tolly and Bagration had personal experience of commanding Jaeger units; these men recognized the need to improve the training and handling of the Russian Army's skirmishers so they could counter the formidable and numerous light infantry fielded by Napoleon.

The Jaeger regiments differed widely in their levels of experience and expertise; generally speaking, those employed in the wars against the Ottomans and the Swedes performed most effectively in 1812–14, often having to operate independently and becoming adept at marksmanship, intelligent use of cover, and rapid movement through difficult terrain – all essential skills in the struggle first to eject Napoleon from Russia, and then to beat his forces in Germany and France.

French

In the years after 1808 Napoleon's conception of the battlefield role of his Imperial Guard appears to have undergone a transformation. In the campaigns of 1805–07 the infantry of the Guard had been a seasoned elite formed from long-service veterans, with an admixture of cadets (known as *vélites* in Napoleonic parlance) intended for leadership roles in the Army. Although these principles survived, from 1809 onwards the newly created conscript regiments of the *Jeune Garde* ('Young Guard') played a far more active battlefield role than their senior brethren, spearheading assaults against the Austrians at Essling (21–22 May 1809) and seeing service in the Iberian Peninsula as part of Napoleon's occupying forces.

This expansion of the Guard stemmed from the need to create a strong, mobile reserve in the absence of the many seasoned troops lost in four years of war, and the desire on Napoleon's part to make military service more attractive to the young men who were compelled to serve the Empire – only the best would be admitted to the Guard. The new regiments, although given colourful titles redolent of a notional light-infantry role, were in fact standard, general-purpose infantry, like their comrades in the Line; while being capable of skirmishing, they were, first and foremost, close-order troops.

On 16 January 1809 the Tirailleurs-Grenadiers (later simply termed Tirailleurs) and Tirailleurs-Chasseurs (later renamed Voltigeurs) were established, but after the Austrian campaign of that year Napoleon decided

OPPOSITE
Four Jaeger personnel, by Richard Knötel. At left is a Jaeger of the 38th Jaeger Regiment, the junior Jaeger regiment of the 9th Infantry Division; the light-blue shoulder-straps are correct, but the '2' on them is not – conceivably a misrendering of the Cyrillic '9'? Second from left is a grenadier of the 1st battalion, indicated by the solid red pompon, three-flamed grenade and black plume; the junior officer behind him wears an NCO's pompon, while the Jaeger NCO at right has the yellow shoulder-straps worn by members of a Division's senior Jaeger regiment. (RC)

LEFT

Tirailleur-grenadier in the pre-1813 full-dress uniform, after Carle Vernet; the red-over-white plume suggests the 1st Tirailleurs. For the invasion of Russia the Young Guard retained the sabre and second cross-belt. The gold stripe on the upper-right sleeve is unusual; long-service chevrons normally appeared on the upper-left sleeve. (RC)

RIGHT

Voltigeur in the full-dress uniform worn before 1813, after Carle Vernet; note the distinctive yellow collar, peculiar to *voltigeurs*. The Guard Voltigeurs were given the privilege of wearing epaulettes, a traditional preserve of elite troops – unlike their colleagues in the Tirailleurs, who had to make do with red shoulder-straps until 1815, when red epaulettes were issued instead. (RC)

further to increase his 'Young Guard' (a title distinguishing the carefully selected conscripts of the new regiments from the veterans of the 'Old Guard'). At the end of 1811 the Young Guard included six regiments each of Tirailleurs and Voltigeurs, plus a regiment of Flanquers. By the time of the invasion of Russia, the Imperial Guard contingent included three infantry Divisions, two of which fielded a total of nine, later 11, Young Guard regiments.

The Russian campaign would decimate the ranks of the Guard as it did the rest of Napoleon's army. In June 1812 the 6th Voltigeurs crossed the River Niemen with 34 officers and 1,535 other ranks, but by 26 December 1812 the unit was just 12 officers and eight men strong. Even so, the evident combat value of the Young Guard prompted Napoleon not only to bring it up to strength again, but to expand it dramatically – to include 13 regiments each of Voltigeurs and Tirailleurs, and a second regiment of Flanquers, after April 1813. Young Guard units in Spain, such as the 2nd Voltigeurs, were recalled to fight in Germany. The vast armies that fought for Napoleon at Leipzig were swelled by fully four Divisions of Young Guard infantry, each complete with its own artillery.

The 1813 campaign also left its mark on the Young Guard, but if anything its importance increased again as the invasion of France loomed: beginning of 1814, Paul de Bourgoing of the 9th Tirailleurs wrote, 'Our regiments had lost a considerable number of their men in the campaign of 1813; the 9th Tirailleurs, after having passed the Rhine, had to be almost completely rebuilt' (Bourgoing 1864: 336). On 21 January 1814 an Imperial Decree ordered the creation of the 14th to 19th regiments of Tirailleurs and Voltigeurs; in addition a third battalion of each Young Guard regiment was to be raised. At Craonne the majority of the French troops employed were Guardsmen, and although the Young Guard's combat effectiveness was waning by April 1814, Napoleon could not have won the dazzling French victories of the 1814 campaign without his Young Guardsmen.

ENLISTMENT AND TRAINING

Russian

The Russian soldier was a conscript, the vast majority of whom were illiterate agricultural labourers, either privately owned serfs or state peasants. Each year (or more frequently in times of crisis) an Imperial Order or *Ukaze* would be sent to each province of the Russian Empire stating the number of men the armed forces required per 500 adult males. Notional height and age regulations were often ignored, meaning those unfit for military service were also enrolled. The clergy, nobility and members of the Jewish community were exempt from conscription, and substitutes could be hired by those able to pay. In 1811, the 81st Levy required three souls per 500, raising 126,392 men; the three levies made in 1812, the year of crisis, required ten, seven and eight souls per 500 respectively, together contributing a staggering 854,139 men. There was no levy in 1813, and in 1814 only one, with only two souls per 500 required.

Families were usually given some power to decide which of their menfolk should go, and so young single men were normally conscripted; in some regiments, however, more than 50 per cent of recruits were married. From 1811, new recruits appear to have joined the 'centre' companies of each battalion, with service in the grenadier company being open only to combat veterans with good character and discipline. Among those conscripted in 1812 was 20-year-old Pamfil Nazarov from Filimonovo in Tver Province. His family was selected to supply one recruit and since he had two older brothers who were married and had children, and his younger brother was too young, it was decided that Pamfil should go. He was taken to St Petersburg, where he entered the 6th Jaeger Company of the Finland Guards Regiment; his height, nearly 1.60m, meant he was selected for the Guard. Leontii Korennoi was married when he joined the Army. At one time serving in a garrison regiment, he later became a member of the 3rd Grenadier Company of the Finland Guards Regiment, but despite his exploits at the battles of Borodino and Leipzig, and his fame afterwards, little is known about 'Uncle Korennoi'.

Training the recruits in standing and marching correctly began immediately, en route to the regiment or depot, often located many hundreds of kilometres away from the recruits' homes to minimize the risks of desertion. From March 1811 each of these depots was linked to a specific infantry Division, which provided personnel to train the recruits destined to join its regiments. (Nazarov was despatched to St Petersburg because the 1st Infantry Division, made up of the six Lifeguard regiments, did not have a depot.)

Russian infantry were trained to move at an ordinary pace (*tchyi shag*) of 60–70 paces per minute,

Russian troops in the field, by Johann Adam Klein, *c.* 1815–16. Note the long greatcoats and full beards worn by two of these men, presumably recruits waiting to be shaved, and the undress cap worn by the barber at work on the left. (ASKB)

a rapid pace (*skoryi shag*) of 100–110 paces per minute, and a 'double pace' (*udwonyi shag*) of 140–160 paces per minute; in addition, skirmishers such as the Jaeger employed a rapid pace – basically a run – of 150–200 paces per minute, in a bid to match the rapid battlefield movement for which their French opponents were justly famed.

Effective close-order firepower also had its roots in the Russian infantry's training regime. The publication *Shkola rekrut ili soldat* ('Schooling for Recruit or Soldier') stressed the importance of accuracy in firing, and infantry were expected to load and fire their muskets at least three times a minute. Like armies across Europe, the Russians placed their close-order infantry in three ranks, and it appears that some effort was made to emulate the French and use the third rank to reload muskets for those in front of them, but not to fire themselves; as in the French Army, this method is likely to have caused confusion on the battlefield.

The realities of wartime meant that parade-ground smartness and formality suffered. Even among the Russian Lifeguard regiments, standards were slipping; the Grand Duke Constantine, the Tsar's brother, wrote in disgust that the war had 'ruined the soldiers … [because] some of the lower ranks among the veterans are already out of practice, while the youngsters have no idea at all how to mount a Regimental Guard' (quoted in Piotrovsky 2005: 221). In one way this was a good thing, insofar that a soldier was no longer an automaton who would be beaten if he showed any initiative, which had made poor-quality Jaeger. Even before 1812 progressive officers allowed their troops to develop as individuals; as early as 1800 Colonel (later General of Infantry) Peter Bagration allowed the soldiers of the Jaeger formation he commanded to use their initiative, and so become more able to match the French skirmishers in battle. By learning through experience due to constant warfare, the Jaeger regiments became more efficient in their drill and tactics, which the veterans passed on to new recruits, meaning that by the time of the 1812 to 1814 campaigns they were able to match, and frequently best, the French skirmishers.

French

The Young Guard was founded on the basis of conscription. Although volunteers were encouraged, of a group of 463 recruits raised for the 1st Tirailleurs only five were volunteers, and just one of a contingent of 200 recruits for the 1st Voltigeurs (Sokolov 2003: 446, 449). The method of conscription was the same as for the Line regiments. Men between the ages of 20 and 25, divided into five classes based on age, could be called up for service; in 1813 men from all five classes were conscripted to replace those lost in Russia – and on 27 September 1813 the classes of 1814 and 1815 were also called up. It was the latter recruits who were known as 'Marie-Louises' after the young Empress, but even the class of 1815 were 19 years old – hardly the young teenagers traditionally associated with Napoleon's armies at this time.

When a decree was issued, those eligible to be conscripted drew lots; those who drew the lowest numbers were conscripted and those drawing higher numbers were either exempted from military service or selected to serve in the National Guard. From 1802 a conscript could hire a replacement, but the vast majority could not afford the expense. Those conscripts selected for the Young Guard had to be able to read and write, so were usually better educated than their counterparts in the Middle and Old Guard. Moreover, since they were more likely to have come from the artisan classes, they may also have been from a better social background. Sous-lieutenant Paul de Bourgoing of the 5th Tirailleurs, raised on 18 May 1811, comments on the ages of his soldiers:

> The oldest of our NCOs, who exemplified the skills of this important position, were twenty-five years old and had four or five years' experience of campaigning. But as for the others, as for our soldiers, our *tirailleurs*, our barely adolescent *sapeurs* [pioneers], as for the *sous-lieutenants* newly graduated from the Ecole militaire, most were barely twenty years old. Several of our drummers from Amsterdam or Frisia were no more than fifteen. (Quoted in Uffindell 2007: 83)

However, by 1813 the Young Guard no longer took the cream of the conscripts, as Général de division Marie-François, Comte Caffarelli du Falga observed that June: 'Each of the *13e Régiments* of *Tirailleurs* and of *Voltigeurs* has more than 1,800 men, who are among the feeblest and puniest men produced by the conscription' (quoted in Uffindell 2007: 89). Some tried to desert at the first opportunity, like 21-year-old Pierre-François Samijn of the 11th Tirailleurs, who deserted twice in three months (Uffindell 2007: 89).

A further source of manpower was the rest of the Guard, and indeed the Army as a whole. Many Young Guard officers, and often NCOs, were transferred between Guard or Line regiments as their careers progressed – or stagnated. This shuffling of personnel helped to spread expertise and standardise the Young Guard's approach to drill and tactics, but may have proved disruptive when officers were rapidly transferred between regiments, as well as possibly fomenting jealousy and rivalry in the officer corps.

In theory the regiments of the Young Guard were better trained than those of the Line, although they followed the same 1791 regulations, known as the *Réglement concernant l'exercice et les manoeuvres de l'infanterie* ('Manual for the training and manoeuvres of the infantry'). Based on the three-deep line to deliver fire, and the widespread use of columnar formations to manoeuvre, these regulations specified an 'ordinary pace' of 76 paces per minute, with each pace being 2 *pied* (roughly

French soldiers receiving uniforms and weapons, by Carle Vernet. The barefooted man in the centre wears the pre-1812 *bonnet de police* (undress cap) on his head; he holds a pair of shoes in his right hand and has slung his cross-belts around his neck. (ASKB)

65cm). Close-order fire could be given by platoon (*feu de peleton*), either direct (straight ahead) or oblique (to the left or right), or by independent files (*feu de deux rangs*), in which the front two ranks fired. Certainly the decision to employ Young Guard units in Spain before the Russian campaign exposed these young soldiers to low-intensity operations and campaign life, thereby toughening them up for the ordeal ahead of them (Uffindell 2007: 50–51).

By 1813, the Saxon staff officer Major Ernst, Baron von Odeleben wrote, 'The Guard was just about the only body of French troops to distinguish itself by its dress and the precision of its manoeuvres' (quoted in Uffindell 2007: 148). Even so, 48 men from the Young Guard were charged with causing self-inflicted wounds to their hands after the battle of Bautzen (20–21 May 1813). Fortunately for them Baron Dominique Larrey, the Imperial Surgeon, found that it was a lack of training that had caused these wounds because the third rank was firing too close to the front rank, so that the ball was grazing the hands of their comrades.

The latter years also saw the incorporation of troops who had served in the armies of France's satellites. On 21 January 1814, the 14th to 16th Regiments of Tirailleurs and Voltigeurs were formed with a cadre of former soldiers of the Spanish Royal Guard that had served Napoleon's brother Joseph, erstwhile King of Spain. The Imperial decree raising these regiments stated that they were to be composed of volunteers between the ages of '20 to 40 or more', although 18- and 19-year-olds were also to be accepted as well as men up to 50 if they were physically fit. These volunteers were to be engaged until the enemy had been driven from French territory. In return their wives and children would receive a pension if their menfolk were killed. By 12 February 1814, 1,500 recruits were already at the Imperial Guard depot, and Joseph wrote to his brother the Emperor reporting that a further 1,000 to 1,500 were arriving daily.

Returning veterans also played a part in fulfilling the Young Guard's manning requirements. In 1814, Bourgoing was appointed to help raise the 3rd Battalion of the 9th Tirailleurs; it was to be organised at Courbervoie, where the 3rd Battalion of the 4th Tirailleurs was also being formed. Such was the shortage of NCOs that the governor of Les Invalides was asked to select those that were the least disabled to join the regiments. Two invalids joined Bourgoing's battalion as *sergents*, who were 'among the best and most active of our NCOs' (Bourgoing 1864: 339). Bourgoing's battalion was then sent to Compèigne, where its men received basic training. However, after just six weeks they were ordered to join the field army.

The training situation was dire by 1814, with Maréchal MacDonald complaining, 'I hardly count on the conscripts of the Young Guard; their officers say that they do not know how to turn to the right and I fear they know the about turn only too well' (quoted in Weil 1892 (II): 2). Boyer de Rébeval recorded that the soldiers of his Young Guard Division at Craonne had 'barely had time to learn how to load a musket'. During the battle his officers had no choice but to leave their men exposed to direct artillery fire, believing that they would run away if they were ordered to retreat.

MOTIVATION, MORALE AND LOGISTICS

Russian

Upon joining his regiment or depot, each recruit was meant to be guided by a *diad'ka* ('uncle'), with at least ten years' service, but brutal discipline relying heavily on corporal punishment was applied. *Ego Imperiatorskago Velichestva Voinskii Ustav o Polevoi Pekhotnoi Sluzhvbe* ('His Imperial Majesty's Regulations concerning Field Infantry Service'), published in 1797, stated that the least mistake by a recruit should not be tolerated and that they should 'exercise as perfectly as an old soldier'. When Nazarov's musket misfired during firing practice he was severely beaten in front of his whole company as an example to the others; he 'collapsed and became ill several times a day' (quoted in Spring 2002: 16). There was a strong move away from corporal punishment, however, at the highest levels; General of Infantry Mikhail Barclay de Tolly believed that 'The Russian soldier has all the highest military virtues: he is brave, zealous, obedient, devoted, and not wayward; consequently there are certainly ways, without employing cruelty, to train him and to maintain discipline' (quoted in Lieven 2010: 108–09).

The decision to revert to provincial or numerical regimental titles, rather than the name of the *shef* (head of the regiment), meant that Russian soldiers found it easier to develop a pride in their unit, although wartime losses diluted this attachment to the regiment. Fedor Shubert, who served as a lieutenant-

Russian soldiers, including a soldier of the 10th Jaeger Regiment, snatch some sleep on a ridge watched over by a sentry of the 38th Jaeger Regiment, also of the 9th Infantry Division, and an officer of the Line infantry; a drawing by Johann Adam Klein, partly hand-coloured by Georg Schäfer. In what may be a colourist's error, the man of the 10th Jaeger Regiment wears the red-piped green shoulder-straps normally associated with the junior Jaeger regiment of each Division after April 1814, the senior regiment taking the light-blue colour previously associated with the junior before that date. Note the baggy campaign trousers worn by the sentry, and the white gaiter-trousers specified for summer worn by the resting soldiers. (ASKB)

This plate depicts a young private soldier of the
19th Jaeger Regiment at Craonne.

Weapons, dress and equipment

This soldier carries the standard 1808-pattern musket (**1**), which had a 17.78mm-calibre barrel and was 114cm long; it weighed about 4.47kg with the socket bayonet (**2**), which was 52cm long. He wears the distinctive 1812-pattern shako (**3**); it has a buckle on the lower rear edge so the diameter can be adjusted (**4**). His oval pompon with a white edge and dark-green centre (**5**) and shako plate with only one flame (**6**) denote a soldier of centre company of the 1st Battalion. Many Russian units wore the shako-cords (**7**) even on campaign.

The Jaeger wore similar uniforms to other Russian infantry, i.e. a dark-green double-breasted coatee, but with a dark-green collar and cuffs piped red. This man wears his greatcoat (**8**) for warmth; single-breasted and made of undyed cloth, it has shoulder straps (**9**) in yellow with the red Divisional number '24'. He has a white brassard

(**10**) tied around his left arm to identify him as a soldier of the Coalition forces fighting against France. Visible beneath his greatcoat are his black winter gaiters (**11**); his shoes (**12**) are square-toed and the same shape for both sides. White gaiter-trousers were worn in the summer months.

He wears black leather diagonal crossbelts (**13**), common to most Jaeger regiments with the exception of some personnel of the 33rd to 46th regiments; these units had formerly been 'musketeer' (line infantry) regiments and so retained their white belts for a time. The cartridge box (**14**) on his rear right hip has the regimental number in brass attached to it. On his rear left hip (suspended on a strap over his right shoulder) he wears a haversack (**15**). On his back he wears a black leather knapsack (**16**) with a metal canteen (**17**) attached to it. All told, his uniform and equipment weighs about 30kg.

colonel on the Russian General Staff in 1812, compared the Russian soldier of that year to his counterpart of 1807:

> Every man knew one thing only … his duty was to hold any position allotted to him to the death … [but] The state of the Russian Army in 1806 lasted more or less until the war of 1812–1814, at which point it was substantially altered. The constant wars had taken away many of the old soldiers, and the young ones did not have the same traditions; nor could they feel the same attachment to their corps as the old ones did. (Quoted in Spring 2002: 42)

The average Russian soldier, enlisted for 25 years – effectively a life sentence – found solace in religious faith, and many seem to have regarded death as a release from their earthly travails. Surrender was not a viable option for Russian soldiers fighting against Ottoman troops or Caucasian warriors in the brutal conflicts along the empire's frontiers. These attitudes daunted their French opponents, as Colonel Charles Pierre Lubin Griois, recalled. 'I could never have imagined that kind of passive courage which I have since seen a hundred times in the soldiers of that nation, which stems, I believe, from their ignorance and credulous superstition … for they die kissing the image of St Nicholas which they always carry with them, they believe they will go straight to heaven, and almost give thanks for the bullet which sends them there' (Griois 1909: II.9).

In 1815 Captain Cavalié Mercer of the British Royal Horse Artillery recorded that as 'smart as they are on the parade' ground, Russian soldiers 'are the dirtiest slovens in the world off it; the usual costume in which one sees them running about la Chapelle is a dirty forage cap, as dirty a grey greatcoat, generally gathered back by the waist-strap, so as to be out of the way, dirty linen trousers, shoved up at the bottom by the projection of the unlaced half boot' (quoted in Spring 2002: 27). These linen trousers were baggy and tied at the ankle by cord or string. However, the 'parade ground' look – smart, clean uniforms – is depicted by artists like Johann Adam Klein of Nuremberg. That is not to say that the Russians did not suffer from severe supply problems. According to Napoleonic veteran and historian Alexander Mikhailovsky-Danilevsky, who served as a staff captain in 1813:

> There was such a scarcity of uniforms and shoes, that out of Prince Eugene of Wirtemberg's [sic] entire corps, it was hardly possible to pick out a thousand men decently enough clothed and shod for this duty. In their exterior, Raiéfsky's troops had more the look of Frenchmen than Russians, as the men, on joining from the reserves in grey jackets, had lost no time in exchanging them for French uniforms, which they stripped from the backs of the killed and prisoners. (Mikhailofsky-Danilefsky 1839: 380–81)

Pamfil Nazarov records that the Tsar wept when he saw the Russian Army were marching in bare feet, having worn out their boots, so new ones were quickly ordered. Nazarov was lucky, being among those who were quickly issued with a new pair.

French

Even more than the rest of the Army, the Imperial Guard revered Napoleon, and his presence with them on campaign provided a boost to morale. Conversely, Napoleon's decision to abandon his army and return to Paris in late 1812 dismayed many of his Guardsmen. Guard regiments enjoyed priority when supplies were available, but led the rest of the Army to feel hatred as well as envy in the wake of the Guard infantry's lack of involvement in the fighting before Krasnyi. By 1814, the Guard had regained some prestige, but the Guardsmen's high-handed behaviour during the Retreat had left a lasting impression.

Although they notionally enjoyed many advantages when it came to supply, the Young Guardsmen stationed in Spain before the Russian campaign had seen plenty of hardship and deprivation, leading them to dub their commanding general, Roguet – 'Général Nada' (Spanish for 'nothing') (Uffindell 2007: 50). On campaign, Napoleonic infantry often presented a ragged appearance. Certainly Leopold Beyer, in his *War Scenes* produced between 1813 and 1815, appears to confirm this when he depicts French infantry wearing worn-out greatcoats and headgear and no shoes. When on parade, entering cities or preparing for battle, however, the soldiers often changed into their parade uniforms so that they could make a magnificent impression. At Smolensk in November 1812 the Hessian Hauptmann Franz Röder saw the Young Guard cleaning their equipment, although he did not know whether there was going to be a parade or a battle.

This is not to say that uniforms did not wear out and a soldier would have to wait for his annual clothes issue, which could be delayed due to supply problems. Newly formed units would be equipped en masse – the recruits of Boyer de Rébeval's 8th Young Guard Infantry Division, for example, received their clothing at Charenton shortly after the Division was formed in February 1814. As was their privilege the Guard would be issued with their uniforms first, although in the mean time they might have to make do with the local cloth to mend or replace items of clothing until then.

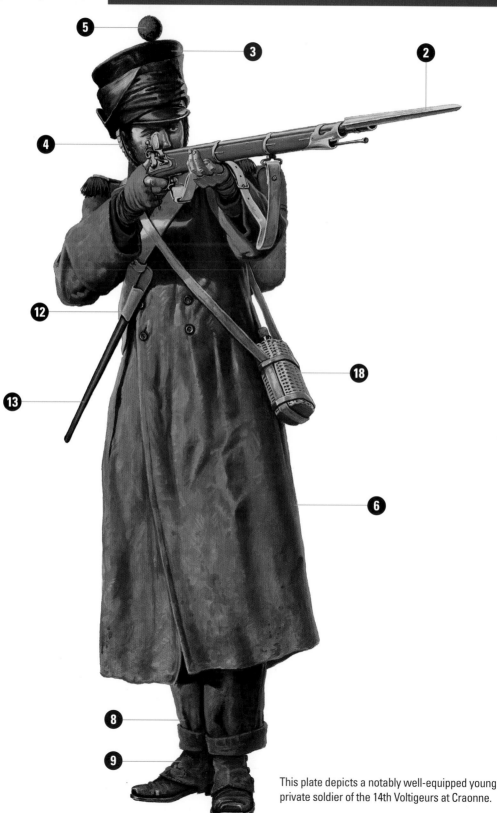

This plate depicts a notably well-equipped young private soldier of the 14th Voltigeurs at Craonne.

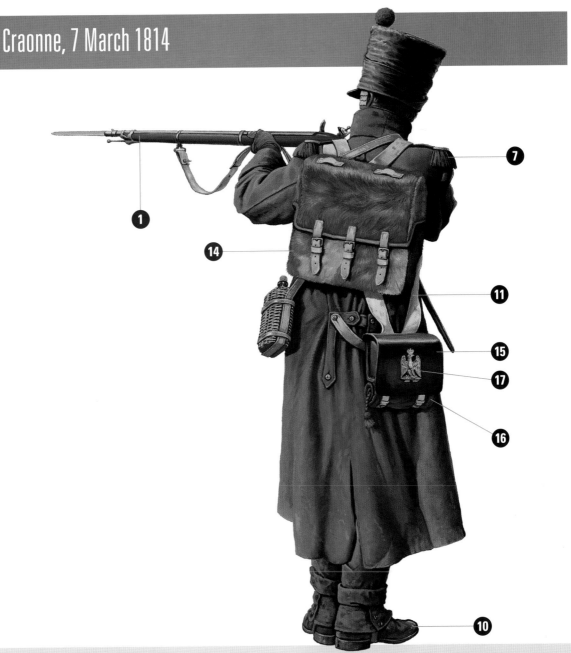

Weapons, dress and equipment

This man carries the standard An IX pattern musket (**1**) with all fittings in iron, unlike the muskets issued to the Old Guard regiments; it was 152cm long and weighed about 4.7kg with the bayonet (**2**), which was 46.5cm long.

His shako (**3**) is covered with an oilskin cover obscuring the cockade and shako plate; it has a leather chinstrap, tied under the chin, with brass scales (**4**) and a spherical pompon (**5**). On parade, the Young Guard regiments had a similar appearance to the Line infantry after 1812, i.e. a lapelled *habit-veste* (jacket) in blue – except for the Flanquers, who wore green – and smart breeches and gaiters. Their buttons bore the imperial eagle instead of the regimental number as worn by the Line regiments. On campaign, however, this colourful uniform was often covered or replaced by the *capote* or greatcoat (**6**),

a voluminous garment – here with *voltigeur* epaulettes (**7**) attached – offering some protection against the elements. Campaign trousers (**8**) are worn over black cloth gaiters (**9**) and shoes (**10**) that are the same shape as each other, as with his Russian counterpart.

He wears a single leather crossbelt (**11**), 70mm wide and with unstitched edges, over his left shoulder; it has a white leather bayonet-frog (**12**) attached to it over his front right hip. The bayonet scabbard (**13**) is covered in brown leather. His knapsack (**14**) is made of calfskin and with its contents weighed about 5.5kg. His cartridge box (**15**) has his rolled forage cap (**16**) beneath it and sports an eagle device (**17**). He wears a canteen (**18**) on a cord; the French Army did not issue a canteen, so this will have been provided by the individual or unit. All told, his uniform and equipment weighs about 26kg.

LEADERSHIP

Russian

While every French soldier supposedly had a marshal's baton in his knapsack, a Russian soldier could only hope to achieve the rank of a senior NCO, after many years of service. If he did become an officer this would ennoble him, which Tsar Paul had all but prohibited. Out of a sample of 2,078 officers taken in 1812, only 32 were peasants and ten were merchants. Even these 32 would have had to serve as NCOs for at least 12 years, and probably did not rise above the rank of ensign or lieutenant. It is said that because of his exploits at Leipzig Leontii Korennoi of the Finland Guards Regiment became an officer, but this is yet to be confirmed.

Even so, in financial terms many Russian officers were worse off than their men, since they had to purchase their own uniforms and food. In 1812, 77 per cent of officers had no estates and did not own any serfs and were unlikely to find their way into one of the more prestigious regiments such as the grenadier regiments or those of the Lifeguard.

Jaeger officers were required to be active and lead by example; the exposed positions often adopted by infantry in a skirmishing role meant that Jaeger officers sometimes had to offer stiff resistance to enemy cavalry to avoid being overwhelmed. Even so, official guidance sought to curb individual initiative on the part of company officers. In the summer of 1812 a document entitled *Nastavlennii Gospodam Pehotahim Ofitseram v den Srazheniya* ('Instructions to the Infantry Officer on the Day of Battle') stated:

> An officer commanding the skirmishers sent in front of the troops may not move his chain forward without permission from his regimental or battalion commander; his duty is to hide his men if possible, but he himself must move incessantly along the chain to supervise his men, observe enemy movements and...cavalry charging at him. Having let them come within 150 paces the officer must [order his men to] fire and, if he sees that he has not stopped them by fire, at a signal he will get his men together in groups of ten back to back. In this position he will continue to fire and stab the approaching horsemen with bayonets in full confidence that his battalion or regiment will rush forward to help them. (Quoted in Zhmodikov & Zhmodikov 2003: II.33–34)

In 1812–1814 many officers came to respect their men, having gone through the hardships of campaign with them. One Russian officer wrote, 'Every day I meet peasant soldiers who are just as good and rational as any nobleman. These simple men have not yet been corrupted by the absurd conventions of our society and they have their own moral ideas which are just as good' (quoted in Spring 2009: 9). Lieutenant-General Mikhail Vorontsov, the Russian commander at Craonne, set up a school in 1815 to teach his men to read and write. However, such conduct may have been the exception rather than the rule.

Detail from an engraving by Georg Adam, *c.* 1814. The Russian infantry officer at left wears his long shako-cords looped around his pompon, a common expedient on campaign, and has shed his knapsack; his colleague at right wears the frock-coat and peaked forage cap favoured by many officers on campaign. Both men have the grey overalls widely worn by infantry officers in the Tsar's army; the colourist has added a red stripe on the left-hand man's overalls, a detail that seems to have become popular in the closing months of the conflict. (ASKB)

French

Although patronage and connections played a part, Napoleon's officers were – at least in theory – promoted on merit, having demonstrated bravery and leadership in battle. Seniority also counted, dating from the day the individual enlisted as a private soldier, then became an NCO and then an officer. Ideally, to become a *sous-lieutenant* the candidate required six years of service, including two as a private and four years as an NCO, but despite heavy losses this was not always the case.

In 1805 Adrien Jean-Baptiste Bourgogne joined the Vélites of the Imperial Guard; he was promoted to *caporal* in 1807 and then *sergent* in 1812. In 1813 he became a *sous-lieutenant* in the newly created 145th Regiment of the Line. Another soldier who slowly worked his way up the ranks was Denis-Epiphane Hure of the 14th Voltigeurs. He enlisted in 1801 and was promoted to *caporal* the following year, but it was not until 1809 that he was promoted to *sergent*, a rank he still held in 1814. Hure was just one of many officers and NCOs of the old Spanish Royal Guard who were appointed to the newly raised Young Guard regiments in 1814.

Some officers and NCOs cared about their men, but others, like Sous-adjudant-major Delaître of the Fusiliers-Grenadiers, who died at Krasnyi, was cruel, 'doing wrong for the mere pleasure of doing it' (Bourgogne 1979: 113). As more Young Guard units were created the harder it became to find good officers and NCOs; in February 1814 some of the battalions in Boyer de Rébeval's Division had just three or four officers and NCOs each.

An unsigned gouache of a *lieutenant* of the Tirailleurs-Grenadiers, c. 1809. Note that the uniform of the senior corps, the Fusiliers-Grenadiers, is being worn by this man, in common with most of the Young Guard's senior officers; the white lapels, here sporting the red ribbon of the Légion d'honneur, must have provided an excellent target for enemy marksmen. (ASKB)

WEAPONS AND TACTICS

Russian

By 1812 the Russian Jaeger carried the same smoothbore muskets as their brethren in the other infantry regiments. At this time the 3rd, 5th, 20th, 21st, 36th and 40th Jaeger regiments are known to have carried imported British muskets. The 31st Jaeger Regiment, serving in the 17th Infantry Division, carried Swedish muskets. Earlier in the Napoleonic Wars, 12 soldiers in each Jaeger company, plus the NCOs, had theoretically been armed with rifles – offering improved accuracy but a slower rate of fire – but these seem to have disappeared from service by 1812. As well as being armed with a musket, members of the grenadier company of each battalion were also equipped with a short sword.

Although Jaeger were trained to operate in close-order formations such as the line and the column – for example, during a skirmish near Craonne on 6 March 1814 Lieutenant Tovbich of the 13th Jaeger Regiment led ten bayonet charges – their primary purpose was to fight in open order. According to the Prussian Regulations of 1794, which were used by other countries:

> The duty of the Tirailleurs [Jaeger] is to hold the enemy at a distance by means of their continual fire. If pressed too hard, the Tirailleurs shall rally on the small troops destined to support them, while those small detachments attempt to drive back the advancing enemy.
>
> While the Tirailleurs are engaged, the officer in charge shall continually watch the enemy and the force he is to cover. He shall pay particular attention to the unit he is defending so that he may coordinate the movements of his forces and to take successive positions, which favour the formation of the line. (Quoted in Nafziger 1996a: 112)

Like skirmishers of other nationalities the Russian Jaeger fought in mutually supporting pairs; one man would wait with loaded musket while the other loaded his weapon, to ensure that one man of the pair was always ready to fire. Jaeger were deployed in a 'chain' across a formation's front. This was similar to the advice given in the 1794 Prussian regulations. Once the enemy's skirmishers had been dealt with, the Jaeger could disrupt the enemy formations by picking off the officers, NCOs and so on.

In 1785 Kutuzov became the commander of the Bug Jaeger Corps and in the following year he wrote *Primetchaniya o Pekhotnoi Sluzhbe Voobsshche I o Yegerskoi Oxobenno* ('Remarks about the Infantry Service in General and about Jaeger in Particular'). These 'remarks' set out how his unit was

Jaeger drummer (left) and hornist (right), by Lev Ivanovich Kiel. Musicians such as these were crucial for disseminating commands and maintaining morale. The drummer appears to be from the marksman platoon of the 1st Grenadier Company, judging by his solid-yellow pompon – although the single-flamed grenade on his shako suggests membership of a Jaeger company – while the hornist, an NCO, wears a white-topped red plume, indicating he belongs to one of his regiment's grenadier platoons, and the usual metallic edging to collar and cuffs in addition to the lace, shoulder wings and sleeve chevrons of his role. Both men carry sabres for self-defence, while the drummer also wears a drum apron. (RC)

to perform and since they were so successful they were adopted by other Jaeger regiments well into the Napoleonic Wars. It was not until 1811 that new regulations were introduced. *Egerskago Ucheniya* ('Jaeger Training') prescribed that when deployed in skirmish order, the front-rank men of the three centre companies of a Jaeger battalion were to form the first chain or skirmish line, and the second-rank soldiers another chain of skirmishers; the third-rank men and the remaining company were to form the reserve. The skirmish line would be sent forward, usually about 57–71m in front of the reserve, with 35–42.5m between chains. There was to be a pace between the two men of each pair and four or five paces between these pairs. The whole skirmish formation would deploy between 142.2m and 355.5m in front of the formation it was protecting (Zhmodikov & Zhmodikov 2003: II.29–30).

By the end of the Napoleonic Wars some Jaeger regiments appear to have adopted single 'chains'. According to Colonel (later Major-General) Sergey Ivanovich Mayevsky, commander of the 13th Jaeger Regiment, on the eve of the battle of Craonne 'half of my platoons stood in a chain; the others were in reserve so that one line reinforced the other' (Maievski 1873: 268–69). However, some traditionalist Russian officers, including the Grand Duke Constantine, appear to have preferred to employ a 'double chain' as late as

Russian 1796-pattern musket, stamped '1804'. Copied from the 1784-pattern Prussian musket, this 19.7mm-calibre weapon was 141cm long and weighed 5kg; the later 1808-pattern, in 17.78mm calibre, weighed a more manageable 4.47kg. Note the brass fittings, the lack of 'belly bands' encircling the barrel and the unusual position of the rear sling-swivel, well behind the trigger-guard. (© Royal Armouries I.2350)

Soldiers of the 39th Jaeger Regiment, October 1815, drawn by Johann Adam Klein and partly coloured by Georg Schäfer. This depicts an intriguing array of different styles of knapsacks, no doubt faithfully reflecting the variety to be seen on campaign in both the Russian and the French armies. The 39th Jaeger Regiment was the junior Jaeger regiment of the 10th Infantry Division. (ASKB)

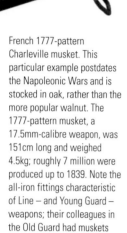

French 1777-pattern Charleville musket. This particular example postdates the Napoleonic Wars and is stocked in oak, rather than the more popular walnut. The 1777-pattern musket, a 17.5mm-calibre weapon, was 151cm long and weighed 4.5kg; roughly 7 million were produced up to 1839. Note the all-iron fittings characteristic of Line – and Young Guard – weapons; their colleagues in the Old Guard had muskets with brass fittings instead. (© Royal Armouries)

1819. Others, though, including Lieutenant-General Ivan Diebitch, regarded this as 'not only useless, but it rather leads to unnecessary casualties and confusion; on the contrary, it is well known that a single chain with [a] reserve may be of great use' (quoted in Spring 2002: 48).

The Russians also employed several unconventional tactics, like playing dead until the enemy had passed, when they would jump to their feet and give a volley into their backs; the 19th Jaeger Regiment did this at Borodino when they were charged by enemy cavalry and did not have time to form square. Bourgogne recalls similar tactics during a night action on the eve of the battle of Krasnyi:

> As the head of our column charged into the Russian camp, we passed several hundred Russians stretched on the snow; we believed them to be dead or dangerously wounded. These men now jumped up and fired on us from behind, so that we had to make a demi-tour to defend ourselves. Unluckily for them, a battalion in the rear came up behind, so that they were taken between two fires, and in five minutes not one was left alive. (Bourgogne 1979: 109)

Jaeger could also fight alongside irregulars. During the pursuit of the Grande Armée in 1812 Jaeger regiments were attached to Cossacks and partisan units, making a deadly combination. The 20th Jaeger Regiment was assigned to the Don Cossacks of Hetman Matvei Platov, while the 11th Jaeger Regiment fought under the command of the partisan leader Lieutenant-Colonel Denis Davidov. Davidov records that he was 'saddened' when he received orders to leave the 11th Jaeger Regiment to guard a river crossing, because 'we were approaching the shores of the Berezina which are covered with woods, and I really could have used an infantry unit' (Davidov 1999: 146). He appealed to General of Infantry Mikhail Miloradovich to rescind the order, but to no avail; even the arrival of two horse-artillery pieces could not compensate Davidov for the loss of his Jaeger regiment.

French

The Young Guard were armed with the same 1777-pattern musket used by the Line, and were initially issued with the infantry sabre, the mark of elite troops (these were officially withdrawn for all except NCOs, drummers and other specialists in 1813). However, with the influx of recruits in 1814 there was a lack of weapons, insomuch that Napoleon suggested that they should be armed with pikes. Whether any found their way onto the battlefield is not known.

The French infantry were – at least in theory – trained to fight in column, in line or as skirmishers irrespective of their regimental title. The regiments of the Young Guard, despite their titles being redolent of light-infantry functions, were employed in much the same manner as the Line infantry. The infantry drew up in a body, usually in three ranks. Although all three ranks could fire in a volley, usually only the first two ranks did so. The men of the third rank either reloaded the muskets of the soldiers of the first two ranks, or they deployed as skirmishers, or they filled the gaps in the formation as it took casualties. However, as one observer recorded, the French were 'famous ammunition wasters' because they fired ineffectually at too long a range (quoted in Muir 2000: 81).

At Krasnyi the Young Guard adopted an unusual two-rank formation, rather than three, due to their numerical weakness – although, according to Hauptmann Röder, the Hessian troops on their flank were drawn up in the usual three ranks (Britten-Austen 1996: 167). Napoleon appears to have favoured the two-deep line, for on 14 October 1813 he wrote to Maréchal Murat, ordering that the infantry of Maréchal Marmont should be deployed in two ranks, 'because the fire and the bayonet of the third rank are insignificant. One of the advantages of this new disposition would be to cause

Three firing postures, according to the 1791 *Règlement*, the drill regulations that were used by the French throughout the Napoleonic Wars. The uniforms here reflect the fashions of a previous generation of soldiers, many of whom were in senior command positions by the time Napoleon invaded Russia in 1812. (RC)

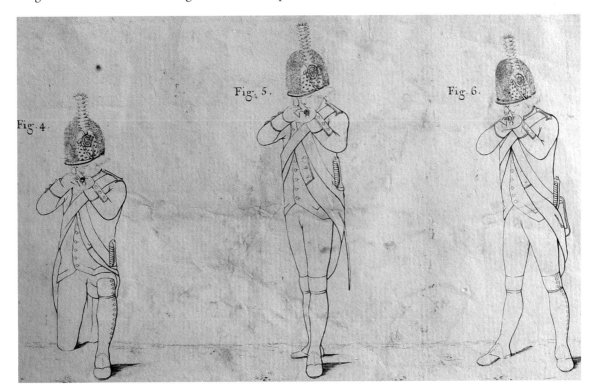

the enemy to believe that the army is one-third stronger than it is in reality' (quoted in Nafziger 1996a: 60). Whether this order was carried out is not known, but using three ranks still appears to have been the preferred option. However, according to Nafziger the French probably had to deploy their infantry in two ranks out of necessity, since the regiments were so weak, although Boyer de Rébeval's 8th Young Guard Infantry Division appears to have been formed in three ranks at Craonne.

When the infantry was to advance it would deploy in a column of attack, which could have a frontage of a single company, two companies or even a full battalion, with the remainder of the battalion, regiment or even Division drawn up behind. The French infantry could be deployed in large columns made up of several battalions; Maréchal MacDonald even deployed 23 battalions in one large column at the battle of Wagram (5–6 July 1809). True, there were intervals between each battalion and the next, but this still meant that these large columns were many ranks deep – at Wagram, 69.

However, the tactician Antoine-Henri de Jomini, who served both Napoleon and Alexander, recommended that columns avoided becoming engaged in a fire-fight, because they could not easily disengage, and lacked firepower. He stated that 'A battalion of eight hundred men, formed in the ordinary manner in a column of four divisions, has about 60 files in each division [i.e. company], of which the first alone – and only the two ranks of that – discharge their pieces. Each battalion would deliver, therefore, 120 shots at a volley' (Jomini 1992: 293).

Instead, the columns usually deployed into line, although if a battalion was caught by enemy forces while deploying it could easily become disorganized and then routed if the necessary enemy forces were available. Furthermore, sometimes the companies drawn up behind the leading company were reluctant to deploy into line, as a British officer observed of his French opponents at the battle of Albuera on 16 May 1811: 'I saw French officers endeavouring to deploy their columns [into line], but all to no purpose; for as soon as the third of a company got out [i.e. emerged], they immediately ran back in order to be covered by the front of the column' (quoted in Arnold 2004: 546). Therefore, skirmishers would protect the column while it was deploying into line. Sometimes a whole battalion might be used as skirmishers. However, the column was also an easy target for enemy artillery and there are accounts of whole files being killed when a column was struck by a cannonball.

Another battle formation was the *ordre mixte*, whereby one battalion was drawn up in a line with a battalion in column at either end. The square formation was employed to receive enemy cavalry, but could also be mobile; Jomini recommended that regimental squares were best for defence against cavalry, whereas battalion squares were best for the offensive. However, by 1814 due to poor training the French infantry probably remained in column throughout the battle, and since most battalions were understrength, several might be combined into one column.

Krasnyi

17 November 1812

BACKGROUND TO BATTLE

On 9 July 1807 Tsar Alexander I and Emperor Napoleon I signed the Treaty of Tilsit, ending the War of the Fourth Coalition, a conflict that had seen the French emperor triumph over the forces of his Habsburg, Hohenzollern and Romanov counterparts in Central Europe. Although at Tilsit the two emperors appeared to be in agreement about the future of European affairs, their relationship steadily deteriorated until war seemed inevitable. Napoleon's strategy was simple. He would invade Russia whose army would 'naturally' meet him in battle somewhere close to the border and he would once again win a glorious victory. On 24 June 1812 Napoleon crossed the River Niemen at the head of his Grande Armée, estimated to have numbered about 530,000, of whom only 232,000 were French. With an army inferior in numbers, the Russian strategy was to retreat in the face of overwhelming odds rather than giving battle as Napoleon had assumed. The long, gruelling march into the Russian hinterland wore down Napoleon's army; a bloody clash at Smolensk (16–18 August) failed to give Napoleon the crushing victory he required, and by 7 September, when the Russians finally made a stand near Borodino, both armies were about even in numbers. However, Borodino was not the decisive battle Napoleon had hoped for and the Russians continued their withdrawal.

Even when Moscow was occupied by the French, the Russians still did not surrender and on 19 October Napoleon

Detail from *Bataille de la Moskowa*, by Pierre Martinet. The infantry of Napoleon's Guard were not committed at Borodino, giving rise to recurrent speculation about what might have transpired had they taken the field at the decisive moment. (ASKB)

Mikhail Illarionovich Golenishchev-Kutuzov (1745–1813), *c.* 1813. Although he is best remembered as the Russian commander at Austerlitz and Borodino, Kutuzov began his military career many years before; he lost his right eye in action against the Ottomans in 1774. He has attracted much controversy over his apparent reluctance to trap Napoleon at Krasnyi, at a moment when the French emperor seemed to be at his mercy. (RC)

was forced to order his men to retreat, intending to follow a route unmarked by the devastation wrought by the invading army's progress towards Moscow. At the battle of Maloyaroslavets (24 October) Napoleon's men won a hard-fought victory but instead of pushing through the Russian forces the French emperor decided to retrace his steps along the route of advance, followed closely by the Russians. The winter and lack of provisions brought misery and death to both armies. It was said that it was the worst winter in living memory, and as one French account records, the very air seemed to freeze. Napoleon's army was hounded by bands of Cossacks and partisans, with Jaeger regiments attached to them and the advance guard of the Russian Army at its heels.

As the Grande Armée briefly sought shelter in Smolensk from 9 November, a large part of the Russian army under General of Cavalry Alexander Tormasov was able to skirt around the city and draw up on the heights east of the town of Krasnyi. Napoleon resolved to make for Minsk – 275km from Smolensk, and the site of a vast French supply depot – and to dispatch his corps in stages rather than massing them for battle. On 16 November the French and Italian troops of Eugène de Beauharnais' IV Corps, the victors of Maloyaroslavets, ran the gauntlet of Russian artillery fire; on the 17th it was the turn of Napoleon's Imperial Guard and Davout's I Corps. The struggle at Krasnyi would quickly become an example in Napoleonic folklore of the fear and admiration provoked in Napoleon's enemies when the French emperor appeared on the battlefield.

On the night of 16/17 November Napoleon exclaimed, 'I have played the Emperor long enough, it is time I played the general' (quoted in Roguet 1865 IV.518). However, according to Général de brigade Philippe-Paul, comte de Ségur, 'Here the enemy's movement were free; ours, fettered; and this genius in the realm of attack was reduced to defending himself' (Ségur 1959: 199). Fortunately for Napoleon and the Grande Armée, the Russians – according to Ségur – were 'overawed by the sight of the conqueror of Egypt and Europe, they did not come to quarters with him. The Pyramids, Marengo, Austerlitz and Friedland seemed to rise up and stand between him and their great army' (Ségur 1959: 199). It is possible that many senior officers in the Russian Army would have agreed with Ségur, but even so they begged Kutuzov to launch an all-out attack on Napoleon, which he refused to do. Even at the time Kutuzov was accused of offering Napoleon a 'golden bridge' out of Russia. However, Kutuzov believed the campaign could still be lost; the Russian Army was also suffering greatly from the severe effects of the winter and many of its soldiers were untried new recruits. Therefore Kutuzov's strategy was to harass the Grande Armée during its long retreat rather than try to destroy it. Moreover, an attack by elements of Général de division François, baron Roguet's 2nd Guard Infantry Division upon forces commanded by Major-General Adam Ozharovsky near Kutkovo during the night of 15/16 November had proved that the Grande Armée could still strike back. The forthcoming engagement would not be a typical battle, therefore, but a series of engagements in which successive elements of the Grande Armée would run the gauntlet of the surrounding Russian forces.

On the 17th, the Russian plan was simple. General of Infantry M.A. Miloradovich, commanding Eugen von Württemberg's II Infantry Corps, Rayevsky's VII Infantry Corps, Uvarov's I Cavalry Corps – less the 1st Cuirassier Division – and Korf's II Cavalry Corps would attack the French to the east of the town; Depreradovich's 1st Cuirassier Division would attack the Grande Armée on the western side. Lieutenant-General D.V. Golitsyn V had under his command Shakhovsky's 3rd Infantry Division of Stroganov's III Infantry Corps, plus Duka's 2nd Cuirassier Division, and was placed in the centre with orders to bombard the French in the town itself. More Russian forces – including those of General of Cavalry A.P. Tormasov, commanding Lavrov's V Infantry Corps, including Major-General K.I. Bistrom's Guards Jaeger Regiment, plus Dokhturov's VI Infantry Corps and Borosdin's VIII Infantry Corps – had been given orders to join Kutuzov near Krasnyi.

However, Kutuzov had given his subordinates strict instructions that they were to harass the enemy as they progressed along the Smolensk Road, rather than cut off the Grande Armée by blocking the route, and ordered that only a few skirmishers should be sent forward. On the other hand Napoleon did not know this, so he sent orders to his Guard to keep the road open until Davout's I Corps and Ney's III Corps had passed through Krasnyi.

The bulk of Roguet's 2nd Guard Infantry Division – the 1st Tirailleurs, Colonel-Major Antoine-Jean-Laurent Mallet's 1st Voltigeurs and the Flanquers – formed the first line around Krasnyi, while the Fusiliers-grenadiers and Fusiliers-chasseurs were posted near Katova. Général de division Henri-François, comte Delaborde's 1st Guard Infantry Division, comprising the 4th, 5th and 6th Tirailleurs and 4th, 5th and 6th Voltigeurs, formed the second line. These two Divisions were supported by the Dutch Guardsmen of the 3rd Grenadiers à pied and the remains of four regiments of Prinz Emil von Hessen's Brigade, which had been part of Victor's IX Corps, but was now attached to the Young Guard.

MAP KEY

1 Early morning: Elements of the Imperial Guard and its attached units deploy east of Krasnyi. Roguet and his fusiliers face Katova; Claparède is posted west of Krasnyi; a battalion of Tindal's 3rd Grenadiers à pied plus wounded and dismounted cavalry barricade Krasnyi. On the bluffs above the River Losmina, Mortier posts Prinz Emil von Hessen's 600 men on the left, the 1st Tirailleurs and 1st Voltigeurs in the centre and a battalion of the 3rd Grenadiers à pied on the right at Voskreseniye; the rest of Delaborde's Division (the Fusiliers-Grenadiers are 250m behind the front line and with the Fusiliers-Chasseurs, with the Old Guard further to the right), plus a squadron of the 2nd Light-Horse Lancers and a Portuguese squadron under the marquis of Loulé, form Mortier's second line.

2 Morning: The Guards Jaeger Regiment and the Finland Guards Regiment, the leading units of the Lifeguard Infantry Division, divide: Colonel P.S. Makarov leads two battalions of the Guards Jaeger Regiment plus elements of the Finland Guards Regiment towards Krasnyi, while the remainder reinforce Golitsyn V or head towards the west of Krasnyi.

3 Morning: Roguet's men drive two battalions of Golitsyn V's infantry from Uvarovo; Kutuzov forbids Golitsyn V from reinforcing Uvarovo; the French in Uvarovo are bombarded with artillery fire. Kutuzov orders Miloradovich to shift his troops to the west and link with Golitsyn V's lines, thereby denying Miloradovich the opportunity to crush Davout.

4 Mid-morning: Davout's I Corps reaches Krasnyi. Bennigsen orders Golitsyn V to recapture Uvarovo; Golitsyn V's attack is met by a simultaneous counter-attack by Guard Voltigeurs; two regiments of Russian cuirassiers attack the Voltigeurs, who form squares, but succumb to a third Russian attack; the French second line falls back under heavy Russian artillery fire.

5 Late morning: The 3rd Grenadiers à pied are driven from their positions by artillery fire; Roguet attempts to support them by attacking the batteries with the 1st Tirailleurs, but this attack fails in the face of artillery fire and cavalry charges.

6 1100hrs (approx.): Napoleon receives reports that Tormasov's troops are readying to march west of Krasnyi; the French Emperor orders the Old Guard to fall back on Krasnyi and then join Eugene's IV Corps in marching west towards Liady and Orsha, and Roguet's Young Guard to remain near Uvarovo until 'nightfall', when it could be relieved by Davout's rallied I Corps; Napoleon departs for Krasnoe.

7 Late morning or early afternoon: Mortier orders Roguet's 3,000 survivors to withdraw towards Krasnyi; they absorb a further artillery barrage as they retreat. Mortier and Davout decide to continue their retreat beyond Krasnyi, leaving only a weak rearguard under Friederich in Krasnyi.

8 1400hrs (approx.): Kutuzov finally allows Tormasov to begin an enveloping movement west through Kutkovo and north to Dobroie; by the time Tormasov completes this manoeuvre at 1600hrs, the Russians' chance to encircle the French will have passed.

9 1500hrs (approx.): Golitsyn V's troops enter Krasnyi; Friederich's rearguard disintegrates.

Battlefield environment

The snow lay thickly on the ground for several days before the clashes at Krasnyi, meaning that on clear nights, the moonlight would show up the movement of large bodies of soldiers against the terrain. Iced-over rivers and streams proved treacherous, as it was hard to tell how secure the ice was, and roads and tracks became especially treacherous as the passage of troops and horses compacted the ice and made it slippery.

Although the Russians appear to have preserved the mobility of their artillery by mounting it upon sledges, the French found that those guns they had been able to save were extremely difficult to move, especially in combat conditions.

Maréchal Ney amid the French rearguard in an illustration depicting the winter conditions, by Adolphe Yvon (note the Guardsman on the right). Many in Napoleon's armies believed the Imperial Guard had aggravated the dire situation facing the French and their allies during the retreat, as personnel of the Guard regiments had looted the supply depots and even attempted to sell the proceeds to their less-fortunate comrades in the Line. (RC)

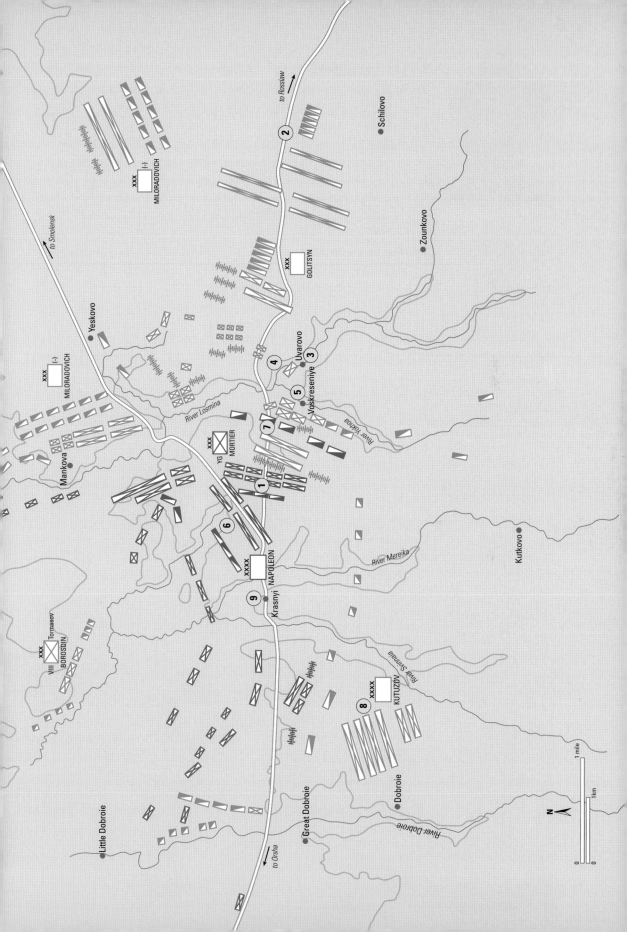

to Rosslaw

Schilovo •

② ⑥⑥⑥⑥⑥

xxx
MILORADOVICH (-)

to Smolensk

Zounkovo •

xxx
GOLITSYN

Yeskovo •

River Losmina

④ Uvarovo ③

⑤ Voskreseniye

xxx
MILORADOVICH (-)

River Vokhoa

⑦

xxx YG MORTIER

Mankova

① ⑥

⑥

xxxx NAPOLEON

River Mereika

⑥

Krasnyi

Kutkovo •

⑨

VIII xxx
Tormasov
BOROSDIN

River Svinmaia

xxxx KUTUZOV

⑧

Little Dobroie •

Dobroie •

to Orsha

Great Dobroie •

River Dobroie

N

1 mile

km

INTO COMBAT

Karl Ivanovich Bistrom (1770–1838). Of noble origins, Bistrom began his military service in the Tsar's Lifeguard; he commanded a series of Jaeger regiments from 1797 onwards, latterly in the Lifeguard. In action against Napoleon's forces in June 1807 he sustained a serious wound to his jaw, which gave him permanent difficulties with his speech. He survived the Napoleonic Wars, fighting at many battles including Krasnyi and Leipzig, and ended his career as a general of infantry. (AM)

Across the snow-covered fields the Young Guardsmen could see the Russian infantry. This was Shakhovsky's 3rd Infantry Division – originally formed from the Reval, Murom, Kopore and Chernigov Infantry regiments, plus the 20th and 21st Jaeger regiments – which positioned itself to the south-east along the Krasnyi–Elnia Road, with two battalions stationed in the town of Uvarovo to await the arrival of the French. However, the 20th Jaeger Regiment had been detached and, though it is known to have been present at the battle, may not have rejoined the Division; in addition, the Selenginsk Infantry Regiment had been transferred from the 23rd Infantry Division. Shakhovsky's infantry were supported by Duka's 2nd Cuirassier Division. (At this time the other Division of III Infantry Corps, the 1st Grenadier Division, appears to have been with Miloradovich in reserve.)

According to Colonel Dezydery Chłapowski, the commander of the 1st Light-Horse Lancers of the Imperial Guard, 'The Russian Tirailleurs advanced in great numbers towards the ravine where we were found and had already taken a small village [Uvarovo] on our right flank' (Chłapowski 1908: 287). Murat ordered Chłapowski's lancers to attack Uvarovo. The snow was too deep for the horses to gallop so they slowly made their way towards the village; as they entered Uvarovo the Jaeger fired at them from the courtyards of the houses, killing four cavalrymen and wounding six others. On reforming his men on the other side of the village, Chłapowski saw a company of the Guard Grenadiers – presumably the 3rd Grenadiers à pied – marching towards Uvarovo, who captured the town without firing a shot. According to the Russian historian Bogdanovich, however, it was soldiers of the Chernigov Infantry Regiment who had occupied the town and were driven from it by elements of Prinz Emil von Hessen's Brigade and the Selenginsk Infantry Regiment and artillery were sent to stabilize the situation.

All this time, according to Capitaine François Dumonceau of the 2nd Light-Horse Lancers of the Imperial Guard, Golitsyn V's artillery had been 'smothering us with projectiles. Fortunately most of them ricocheted on some slight undulation of the terrain and then bounced well over our heads, or else, merely rolling up to us, were spotted and easily avoided. His shells exploded with a crash the more sonorous for the repercussions from the frozen ground' (quoted in Britten-Austin 1996: 166–67). Not all the shots missed their targets, but ploughed into the ranks of the Young Guard. As Ségur records: 'The young soldiers, half of whom were seeing action for the first time, stood up to the deadly fire for three solid hours without taking a step backward or making a movement to get out of its way, and without being able to return it, as their cannon had been destroyed' (Ségur 1959: 199). According to Bourgoing, Delaborde tried to encourage his men by walking 'slowly along the battle front, saying, "Come, my children, let us raise our noses when we smell the powder for the first time." Shouts of joy and cheers greeted these words' (Bourgoing 1864: 196). Napoleon could also be seen, pacing up and down. The French artillery returned fire, but due to supply problems they quickly ran out of ammunition, and so Roguet was forced to send the guns to the rear. Several Napoleonic soldiers who wrote their memoirs record that when they were under artillery fire such as this, they could see the cannonballs coming towards them. Certainly in the close formations where Napoleonic soldiers stood shoulder to shoulder with their comrades it would be difficult to avoid their impending death or being maimed.

At about 1100hrs the leading elements of Davout's I Corps appeared on the Smolensk Road; this brought some relief to the Young Guard because the Russian fire turned on this new threat. Davout's men were surrounded by Cossacks under the command of Major-General V.V. Orlov-Denisov. However, seeing Krasnyi, the survivors of I Corps broke ranks and rushed towards the town, no doubt being pursued by the Cossacks all the way. It was only when they reached the Young Guard that, according to Ségur, Davout and his generals could rally them. They drew up north of the Smolensk Road.

With the arrival of Davout's corps, and news that the Russians were deploying west of Krasnyi Napoleon decided that he would withdraw with his Old Guard. The exact time when Napoleon left is unknown: some sources say the late morning, while others say some time during the afternoon. Whatever time it was, according to Ségur, Napoleon took Mortier's hand and said,

> 'There is not a minute to lose! The enemy is breaking through on every side, Kutuzov may reach Liady, even Orsha and the last bend of the Dnieper before me. I must move rapidly with the Old Guard to occupy that passage. Davout will relieve you. Together you must try to hold out at Krasnoe until nightfall. Then you will rejoin me.' (Quoted in Ségur 1959: 199–200)

On the other hand, Bourgoing claims that Napoleon said to Mortier, 'I leave you here with confidence. You will be attacked by the van of the Russian Army. I ask you to hold out for a whole day. Its advance must be held back as long as possible. I shall be grateful for every hour you gain' (quoted in Bourgoing 1864: 194). The Russians watched as Napoleon and his Old Guard departed. His presence had been the only thing stopping the Russians from advancing and now they renewed their attack with vigour. Kutuzov's chief-of-staff, General of Cavalry Leontii Bennigsen, ordered Golitsyn V to recapture Uvarovo, while Miloradovich's force would attack Davout's I Corps.

On the previous evening elements of the Russian Lifeguard Infantry Division had bivouacked on snow-covered fields 5km from Krasnyi in freezing temperatures. Like the soldiers of the Grande Armée, when they could get wood the Russians would light fires; when they faced the fire their backs would become frozen, so they had to keep turning around all night to keep themselves warm. To some it probably came as a relief when reveille was sounded to form up again; others were probably too exhausted or frozen to care, and would freeze to death. The Finland Guards Regiment and the Guards Jaeger Regiment led the way, marching along the Rosslaw–Krasnyi

Adolphe Édouard Casimir Joseph Mortier (1768–1835), *c.* 1812. Mortier entered the French Army as a *sous-lieutenant* in 1791 and rose to become one of the first group of senior commanders to be created *maréchal d'Empire* by Napoleon, in 1804. After high-profile service as a corps commander in Central Europe and Spain, he led the Young Guard in Russia, a role he reprised in 1813–14 at a host of battles, from Lützen right through to Paris. After a short period of disgrace after Napoleon's defeat he returned to public life and even served briefly as France's ambassador to Russia, before being killed aged 67 in an unsuccessful assassination attempt on France's last king, Louis-Philippe. (RC)

Road. On the eve of the battle of Borodino, the Guards Jaeger Regiment had failed to post pickets despite being in a forward position, so when the French attacked them many were still asleep and so the regiment was driven from its position in disorder; only the 1st Jaeger Regiment saved the Guardsmen from a total rout. Now, as they marched to the sound of the guns at Krasnyi, this was the first opportunity they had to redeem their honour.

However, despite being just a few kilometres from Krasnyi they made slow progress in the knee-deep snow. Near the village of Schilovo, they divided: the 2nd and 3rd Battalions of the Guards Jaeger Regiment, under the command of Colonel Peter Stepanovich Makarov, and at least one company of the Finland Guards Regiment continued to march towards Krasnyi. Makarov appears to have had orders to deploy his two battalions between Golitsyn V and Miloradovich; however, he appears to have left the Finland Guards Regiment company and at least one Guards Jaeger Regiment company with Golitsyn V. Meanwhile, the 1st Battalion of the Guards Jaeger Regiment and the remainder of the Finland Guards Regiment cut across the fields so that they could deploy west of Krasnyi. Their progress was even more delayed because at one point the men of this force had to march in single file because the trackways were so narrow. It would take some time for this force to cover the ground and deploy near the town of Dobroie.

Early in the morning the 3rd (Dutch) Grenadiers had taken up position on the high ground near Uvarovo, but now they were being cut to pieces by Russian artillery. Finally they were forced to abandon their position, which the Russians immediately occupied with their artillery and a screen of Jaeger. With this high ground in Russian hands their guns could now fire upon the Smolensk Road. With the capture of Uvarovo, Golitsyn V's troops were also able to advance past the town and deploy closer to the Young Guard.

According to Ségur, 'Roguet, who was being cut to pieces by [the Russian] fire thought he could silence it. The first regiment he ordered to charge the guns was repulsed' (Ségur 1959: 200). Dumonceau and Bourgogne also record that a regiment was sent forward to recapture the heights, but failed. Unfortunately none of these eyewitnesses records which regiment this was. However, according to Roguet it was the Flanquers, under the command of Colonel Pierre Boudan de Pompejac: 'I pushed forward the regiment of Flanquers. This intrepid band could not make any progress and the division continued to be overwhelmed by enemy artillery' (Roguet 1865 IV: 522).

Seeing that the Flanquers were faltering, Roguet ordered the 1st Voltigeurs to advance. Ségur continues: 'The second [regiment], the 1st Voltigeurs, drove into the very centre of the Russians. Two cavalry charges did not halt them. They pushed steadily on' (Ségur 1959: 200). Roguet records, 'As they advanced the *voltigeurs* were charged by Russian cuirassiers. They formed square and managed to repel two charges before Russian artillery opened fire with case-shot at close range. The cuirassiers made a third charge' (Roguet 1865 IV: 522).

However, according to Capitaine Toussaint Phillip of the Flanquers, the 1st Voltigeurs advanced on the enemy in square, but when they were within pistol range of the Russians, the artillery opened fire with case shot and then they were charged by cuirassiers. Seeing the difficulties that the Flanquers and 1st Voltigeurs were in, and that more Russian cavalry were amassing to attack them, Roguet decided to order them to 'retreat by echelons; the regiment of Flanquers, less exposed, would protect the withdrawal movement of the other. The colonel of the Flanquers, seeing the Voltigeurs also committed, despaired of support and he retreated' (Roguet 1865: IV.523). Phillip continues:

> … our regiment was responsible for the support [of the 1st Voltigeurs] but was forced to retreat after having left on the field of battle two officers and more than 200 men, which reduced the force to about 300 men. M. Pompejac, our colonel and M. Hellier, lieutenant-colonel, had their horses killed under them; several officers were wounded; I received a shot in my greatcoat. (Phillip 1845: 15)

Four soldiers of the Guards Jaeger Regiment, all wearing the 1812 shako with double-headed eagle plate and Lifeguard lace to collar and cuffs. Seated at left is a senior officer, distinguished by his fringed epaulettes and spurred knee-boots; standing to attention next to him is a Jaeger wearing dark-green winter breeches and gaiters, and equipped with side-arm only. Behind the Jaeger is a fully kitted-out soldier of the grenadier platoon, sporting the distinctive long, thin black plume and wearing summer white gaiter-trousers; on the right, supervising the grenadier's fire, is an officer of the grenadier platoon, wearing knapsack, waist-sash, overalls and the fringeless epaulettes of his rank. (AM)

The Voltigeurs' fate was not just sealed by the Russian cuirassiers, however; one French account records that 'Golitsyn sent his cuirassiers into a charge against the Regiment of Voltigeurs of the Guard and also sent some infantry to support' (quoted in Vionnet 2012: 160). According to the Finland Guard Regimental history, 'The 1st French Voltigeur Regiment was completely destroyed by the bayonets of a company of the Guard Jaegers and of the Finland Guard Regiment' (Rostkovski 1881: 142).

The Murom and Reval Infantry regiments also charged the 1st Voltigeurs' square. A soldier of the Reval Infantry Regiment was able to capture the *fanion* (standard) of the 1st Voltigeurs, which was one of 11 French *fanions* and eagles lost at Krasnyi (Andolenko 1969: 279–80). Paul de Bourgoing recorded that he could hear 'the voices of our 20-year-old conscripts, their usual war cries, cries of devotion to the sovereign [Napoleon] mingling with redoubled cheers of the assailants then in no time a gloomy silence' (Bourgoing 1864: 198). Hearing the death throes of the 1st Voltigeurs, Delaborde said, 'The brave

Death in the snow at Krasnyi

RUSSIAN VIEW: Here we see soldiers of a marksman platoon of the Guards Jaeger Regiment (left), firing as they move up towards the beleaguered Young Guardsmen of the 1st Voltigeurs; to the left is a Russian artillery battery and on the right are horsemen of the Novgorod Cuirassier Regiment bearing down on the French formation.

Encumbered in the deep snow by their thick, single-breasted greatcoats and gloves, these marksmen are operating in pairs, in common with standard open-order doctrine; one man in each pair waits with weapon loaded while the other reloads his musket.

Period illustrations often show Russian soldiers wearing full shako ornaments even on campaign; the NCO shown here has looped his shako-cords around the pompon, a common practice. Note the regimental cipher on the cartridge-box and the late-pattern muskets with brass 'belly-bands'.

FRENCH VIEW: The view from the perspective of the French formation is grim indeed; cavalry bear down from the left, while advancing Jaeger personnel add to the fire inflicted on the French by the artillery battery on the right. Exposed and vulnerable, the ragged French formation is at the mercy of the Russians, who – given the mobility of their artillery even in winter conditions, unlike that of the French – are able to practise combined-arms tactics to defeat their enemy.

The French are encumbered by full campaign dress, plus any additional layers they have been able to get; in 1812 the Voltigeurs (and Tirailleurs) retained the sabre, carried on a second cross-belt passing over the right shoulder.

At this stage of the battle the two-deep firing line specified by the Young Guard's commanders is beginning to loosen; each man is firing independently, although one or two have reverted to their training and are attempting to pass their muskets back to have them reloaded.

young men, the poor children; they are still resisting the enemy' (quoted in Bourgoing 1864: 199). Mortier ordered that the 1st Voltigeurs should be recalled, and a messenger was despatched. He found a lieutenant with a blood-soaked face from a sabre cut and asked 'Where is the 1st Voltigeurs?' only to receive the answer: 'They no longer exist; the enemy pursues only a few groups of unfortunate fugitives who defend themselves against the cavalry' (quoted in Bourgoing 1864: 199). A few shots were again heard in the distance and then nothing.

At some point the 1st Tirailleurs also appear to have been ordered forward; Phillip recalls they were ordered to advance on the Russian guns, 'by several battalions marched in echelon, which was the principal manoeuvre in the circumstance' (Phillip 1845: 15). According to Bourgogne, the 1st Tirailleurs

… sent forward as far as the [Russian] batteries, but was stopped by a body of cuirassiers. It then retired to the left of the battery, forming into a square. The enemy's cavalry came onto the attack again, but were received by a heavy fire, which killed a great many. A second charge was made, and met with the same reception. A third charge, supported by grapeshot was successful. The regiment was overwhelmed. The enemy broke into the square and finished off the remainder with their swords. These poor fellows, nearly all very young, having their hands and feet mostly frost-bitten, had no power to defend themselves, and were absolutely massacred. We witnessed the scene without being able to help our comrades. Eleven men only returned; the rest were all killed, wounded, or taken prisoners, driven by sword-thrusts into a little wood opposite. The Colonel covered with wounds, was made prisoner, with several other officers. (Bourgogne 1979: 115)

French troops – from their uniforms, Line infantry – confront Russian cuirassiers in the snow at Krasnyi in this work, completed at least 50 years after the battle, by French artist Alfred Paris. Here we see a glimpse of how close-order infantry sought to repel enemy cavalry by massed fire; the field of view afforded to the mounted senior officer is appreciably better than that enjoyed by his men, demonstrating that remaining mounted in combat was crucial for commanders of infantry regiments and battalions serving on both sides. (RC)

(This colonel, whom Bourgogne calls 'Luron', was probably Colonel-Major August-Nicolas Lenoir, who commanded the 1st Tirailleurs and is known to have been captured during the battle.)

Makarov's 2nd Battalion probably advanced towards the rearguard of Davout's I Corps, while the 3rd Battalion appears to have supported the cuirassiers attacking the 1st Tirailleurs, because Major-General Aleksey Ermolov records that 'Parts of Napoleon's Young Guard and the corps of

Davout fought resolutely, but they could not withstand a vigorous attack by the Life Guard Jaegers' (Yermolov 2005: 199). Bennigsen also records the attack on the 1st Voltigeurs and 1st Tirailleurs:

> Two weak battalions of the Young Guard advanced to cover the main road, the one in front of the position occupied by General Tormassov and the other in front of that of Prince Golitzin. The first was attacked by a battalion of our chasseurs [Jaeger] of the Guard and the second by a battalion of our regiment of Reval. The two enemy battalions … [were either] killed or taken and the rest dispersed. (Quoted in Spring 2009: 219)

Unfortunately, the Regimental History simply records that the 2nd and 3rd Battalions charged a French 'column of 1,200 men which was completely destroyed by the jaegers and the cuirassiers' (Anon. 1896: 91).

Slowly the sounds of musketry died away and there was silence. According to Colonel Louis-Joseph Vionnet de Maringoné of the Fusiliers-Grenadiers, the 'first two regiments of Tirailleurs and Voltigeurs had [already] been entirely wiped out. Of those two units not 120 men were left' (quoted in Britten-Austin 1996: 171). The failure of the Young Guard to recapture the heights overlooking their position allowed the Russian artillery to continue to pound their ranks. Bourgogne records that 'By two o'clock we [the Fusiliers-Grenadiers] had lost a third of our men, but the Fusiliers-Chasseurs were the worst off of all, as, being nearer to the town, they were exposed to a more deadly fire' (Bourgogne 1979: 116). With the Russians closing in upon the French it was decided that if the army was to survive then they had no choice but to abandon Ney's III Corps to its fate, if indeed it still existed.

Exactly when the order was given to retreat is not known: the Young Guard regiments were ordered to withdraw first. The Guard was followed by Davout's corps, which was by now being pressed on all sides. Still Kutuzov did not give the order to advance upon Krasnyi until he was certain that the French were in full retreat. As the Young Guard marched through Krasnyi they were met by a hail of grapeshot from Russian artillery, which had been brought forward on sledges. The French guns tried to keep the Russians at a distance, but it was no use. According to Paul de Bourgoing, 'the main street was swept by musketry' (Bourgoing 1864: 201). The streets were also choked with French stragglers, making the withdrawal difficult. Therefore it was decided that the wounded had to be abandoned. As they emerged from Krasnyi the French found Tormasov's force waiting for them and the Guard were again met by a hail of cannon fire, which inflicted heavy casualties on them: 'every one of the enemy's shots found its mark, the shells could not miss or pass over and every one of them killed or blew the legs off those in the way, wounding those when the impact of the shell was deflected by dead bodies' (Vionnet 2012 :107).

By now the three battalions of the Finland Guards Regiment had deployed in skirmish chains to the west of Krasnyi, and began to fire at the French streaming out of the town. They then advanced upon the French with the

bayonet, but the Young Guard seem to have managed to escape, leaving many of the stragglers of I Corps to be captured, along with Davout's baggage – including his *maréchal*'s baton.

During the battle the Young Guard had suffered greatly: the 1st Voltigeurs had seven officers killed and a further five mortally wounded, with 12 officers suffering injuries including Mallet and both his battalion commanders. Mallet would survive the Russian campaign to incur wounds at the battles of Lützen and Dresden; after joining the 2nd Chasseurs à pied as its commanding officer in December 1813, he was again gravely wounded at Montmirail and subsequently died on 27 February 1814. Unfortunately, no casualty return for the Guard's rank and file appears to have survived, but they were particularly heavy among the 1st Voltigeurs, who had been badly cut up during the battle.

No casualty figures for Golitsyn V's force are known to have survived either, although the regimental history of the Finland Guards Regiment reports that one officer, seven NCOs and 57 private soldiers were wounded, and Colonel Count Alexander Alexandervich Grabovski of the 1st Battalion, one NCO and 21 privates were killed. At this time the regiment was about 700 strong, so a total of 12.28 per cent became casualties (Rostov 1881: 139). In the Guards Jaeger Regiment, just one officer and 24 men were wounded and eight men killed; even so, they managed to capture 31 officers and about 700 other ranks, plus two flags and many carriages (Anon 1896: 91). In all, Kutuzov reported, the total number of Russian casualties were 2,000 killed and wounded.

Both sides claimed the battle as a victory. Napoleon said that he had achieved his task in saving Davout's corps, although the original intention had been to save Ney's as well. Kutuzov claimed a 'decisive victory', because he had badly mauled the Grande Armée, but many Russian officers believed that the French should have been destroyed. Ermolov blamed Kutuzov for the 'indecisive and sluggish actions of our army' (Yermolov 2005: 202). However, Bourgoing believed the battle could be seen as a turning point, in that after it the Grande Armée would become more dispersed as more and more soldiers died and discipline broke down. The French still had to cross the Berezina and after Napoleon's departure for Paris, even his Old Guard would lose cohesion.

Bataille de Krasnoi, 18 Novembre 1812, by Jean-Antoine-Siméon Fort. Depicting the continuing action at Krasnyi two days after the Young Guard's fateful stand, this work shows greatcoat-clad French infantry in close-order columnar formation advancing uphill towards Russian positions shrouded in smoke; the weather conditions and lack of battlefield visibility are well conveyed in this atmospheric painting. (© The Art Gallery Collection/Alamy)

Leipzig

16 October 1813

BACKGROUND TO BATTLE

In December 1812 the majority of the Young Guard regiments that had served in Russia existed on paper only, having succumbed to the various battles, such as Krasnyi, and the Russian winter. The Russian Army had also suffered badly; for example, by early January 1813 the five regiments that formed the 13th Infantry Division – including the 13th and 14th Jaeger Regiments – together numbered only 1,091 (Beskrovnogo 1956: V.22). Kutuzov argued that the Russian Army should wait before it advanced into Germany, but Tsar Alexander was impatient; he did not want Napoleon to be able to recoup his losses, so he ordered the Russian Army to continue its pursuit of the Grande Armée. It would be Alexander's enthusiasm in the forthcoming campaigns that would eventually lead to Napoleon's defeat in 1814.

The Russians scored an early success on 7 February 1813 when they occupied Warsaw. However, the Tsar needed allies if he was to accomplish his aim of liberating Europe. The Prussians declared war on Napoleon on 13 March 1813, eager to revenge their defeat in 1806 and humiliation at Tilsit the following year. This might not have proved disastrous for Napoleon, because he had fought a war against

Prussia and Russia before and won. However, the 1812 campaign had cost Napoleon the lives of many of his veterans. True, his regiments had suffered casualties in previous campaigns, but nothing on this scale – and there had always been sufficient veterans left as a nucleus around which the units could be rebuilt. Furthermore, there had always been a period of peace after a campaign in which he could train the recruits to the standard expected in the Grande Armée. Now, in 1813, the recruits had to be trained on the march to join the field army, rather than at the regimental depots.

Napoleon also recalled regiments from Spain and cleared the depots of the Young Guard and line regiments and so was able to rebuild his army, which outnumbered the combined Russo-Prussian Army. However by weakening the army in Spain, this took some of the pressure off Wellington's and the Spanish Armies. In addition to the loss of men was the loss of horses for the cavalry, which could not be so easily replaced. It would be a lack of cavalry that would hinder Napoleon in the forthcoming campaign.Reinforcements were also on their way to the Russian Army, but they would take time to cover the vast distances between their initial rendezvous and the main army; by mid-April 1813 the Russian II Infantry Corps only numbered 6,109 officers and men, while the IV Infantry Corps had just 2,990 all ranks (Beskrovnogo 1956: V.514–15).

The struggle for Germany started well for the Allies when they defeated the French at Möckern (5 April 1813), but on 28 April Kutuzov died. He was replaced by General of Cavalry Peter Wittgenstein, who although less capable than other senior Russian officers was the most popular choice, having protected St Petersburg from MacDonald's X Corps and Oudinot's II Corps in 1812.

Général de division Pierre Dumoustier's Young Guard Division, which had mustered 11,670 combatants on 25 April, was heavily involved in the fierce fighting at Lützen (2 May), a victory for Napoleon; it suffered 1,069 casualties, including Colonel-Major Jean-Paul-Adam Schramm, commanding officer of the 2nd Voltigeurs, and both majors of the 1st Voltigeurs (Lachouque & Brown 1997: 294). According to Chef de Bataillon Felix Deblais of the 1st Tirailleurs, 'All the Young Guard did marvels', and Joseph Duffraisne of the Fusiliers-Grenadiers recorded, 'It was the Voltigeurs of the Guard who won this battle. They lost many men, up to fifty or sixty per company' (quoted in Uffindell 2007: 94). By 5 May Dumoustier's Division mustered 7,865 combatants; a further 3,040 were in hospital, although only 10 per cent of these were battle casualties, 'a strategic consumption loss of approximately 25 percent from April 25 to May 5' (Bowden 1990: 90).

The Russian Lifeguards were also present at Lützen, and also the subsequent battle of Bautzen (20–21 May), another French success; because of the gallant conduct of his Finland Guards Regiment at Bautzen, Colonel Maxim Constantinovich Kryzhanovsky was promoted to major-general, while his battalion commanders and lesser officers received bravery awards, along with five other ranks in each company (Gulevich 1906: 290). Both Lützen and Bautzen could have been decisive victories for Napoleon, but his lack of cavalry

Major-General Maxim Constantinovich Kryzhanovsky (1777–1839) was the commander of the Finland Guards Regiment from its inception as the Imperial Militia Battalion in 1807 until 1816. He fought at Borodino, Krasnyi, Lützen, Bautzen and Kulm, before being gravely wounded at Leipzig. (AM)

General of Infantry Mikhail Bogdanovich Barclay de Tolly (1757–1818). One of Russia's best senior commanders, Barclay de Tolly served in a succession of Jaeger units in the 1790s before distinguishing himself in the campaigns of 1806–07 and then against the Swedes in Finland in 1808–09. His caution in 1812 – and his German–Scottish ancestry – made him many enemies in the Russian high command, but his proven abilities saw him return to senior command in May 1813. (RC)

had prevented his army routing the Allied forces and they were able to withdraw in good order.

On 18 May the Swedes – under Napoleon's former *maréchal*, Jean-Baptiste-Jules Bernadotte, now the Crown Prince of Sweden – landed in Pomerania on the Allies' side. On 26 May Wittgenstein was replaced by General of Infantry Mikhail Barclay de Tolly. It had been Barclay de Tolly's strategy of retreating into the heart of Russia which – although it had been extremely unpopular – had reduced the strength of Napoleon's Grande Armée. On the same day another clash came at Haynau, but despite the French being defeated, the Allies fell back into the Prussian province of Silesia.

By now both sides were exhausted. Napoleon had made approaches for a ceasefire before the battle of Bautzen, but these had been rejected by Alexander. Now, with Austrian mediation, both sides agreed to an armistice on 4 June, which would last until 16 August. This gave both sides time to recover before the resumption of the campaign. During this period reinforcements arrived to reinforce the Finland Guards Regiment; one 463-strong contingent included Pamfil Nazarov, who had finished his training. This brought the regiment up to about 1,400 strong and so it was able to be formed into three battalions once more (Gulevich 1906: 291). The Grande Armée was also able to increase its strength; by 15 August the 1st to 4th Young Guard Infantry Divisions mustered 8,590, 8,186, 8,037 and 7,894 officers and men respectively (Bowden 1990: 126).

During this armistice the Austrians signed the Treaty of Reichenbach on 27 June, which would lead to Austria declaring war on Napoleon on 12 August. It was decided that each of the main Allied armies would be a mixture of nationalistics. The Army of Bohemia was to be commanded by the Austrian Feldmarschall Karl Philipp, Fürst zu Schwarzenberg; the Army of the North was led by the Crown Prince of Sweden, while the elderly Prussian General der Kavallerie Gebhard Leberecht von Blücher was to command the Army of Silesia. The Allies agreed to the Trachenberg Plan (15 August), which aimed to defeat Napoleon's *maréchaux* one by one, before confronting Napoleon himself. If one of the armies was threatened by Napoleon, then it would retreat, allowing the other two armies to take the initiative.

With the resumption of hostilities this plan worked well, with a string of Allied victories at Großbeeren (23 August), Katzbach (26 August), Hagelberg (27 August), Nollendorf (29–30 August), Kulm (29–30 August), Dennewitz (6 September) and Wartenberg (3 October). True, Schwarzenberg was defeated by Napoleon at Dresden (26–27 August) – where the Young Guard saw action, as well as the Finland Guards Regiment – but slowly Napoleon was being ground down. Moreover, once-loyal allies of the Emperor changed sides; Bavaria, which had been France's ally for centuries, joined the Allies on 8 October, so weakening Napoleon further. Finally the Allies felt strong enough to confront Napoleon at Leipzig. The ensuing battle would be the largest until World War I and a decisive turning point in the struggle between Napoleon and his enemies.

INTO COMBAT

At dawn on 16 October, the Russian Lifeguard and Prussian Royal Guard, about 14,000 strong, were in reserve at Rötha, about 10km (two or three hours' march) to the south of the Allied left wing. All four Young Guard infantry Divisions, grouped into two corps under Maréchaux Oudinot and Mortier, were located behind and to the north of Lauriston's V Corps, which was deployed between Wachau and Liebertwolkwitz (Smith 2001: 69). Both the Young Guard and the Russian Lifeguard would be held in reserve for much of the day.

As the Allied armies were pushed back, Oudinot's corps with other elements of the Imperial Guard and a large formation of cavalry were ordered to take up a position near Meusdorf Farm. Napoleon ordered Oudinot to capture Auenheim Farm, while Mortier's II Young Guard Corps and Lauriston's V Corps were to capture the Universitätsholz. Once these positions had been seized, Murat with his cavalry was to move forward and roll up the lines of the Army of Bohemia. Therefore these positions had to be held by the Allies at all costs.

The French pounded the Allied positions with their massed artillery. According to one Russian officer, 'all hell was really let loose. It seemed impossible that there could be any space between the bullets and the balls which rained onto us' (quoted in Smith 2001: 95). Shortly after 1400hrs, Général de division Bordesoulle's 1st Heavy Cavalry Division advanced, supported by French infantry. According to the Russian officer, 'From the direction of the front came a dull, deep rumbling noise, like the rattling of a thousand heavy chains. It was the sound of hooves and weapons' (quoted in Smith 2001: 96). Murat's cavalry hit Eugen von Württemberg's II Infantry Corps to the north-west of Güldengossa, while the infantry of Lauriston's V Corps attacked Lieutenant-General Andrey Gorchakov's I Infantry Corps to the north-east. Général de division Maison's 16th Infantry Division of Lauriston's V Corps was to capture Güldengossa itself.

The three Prussian battalions garrisoning the town put up a stiff resistance, but were pushed back through the streets and houses of Güldengossa. However, the St Petersburg and Tauride Grenadier regiments of Major-General P.N. Choglokov's 1st Grenadier Division soon arrived, and after heavy fighting forced Maison's 16th Infantry Division to withdraw.

The fight for Wachau, by Richard Knötel. Here Polish troops fighting for Napoleon attempt to storm an imposing building in the village; the confusion and poor visibility prevalent in this sort of combat are well conveyed. Wachau resisted the Coalition forces' assaults on 16 October, but was later abandoned by Napoleon's men. (RC)

MAP KEY

1 0800hrs: Eugen von Württemberg, having deployed his forces north of Güldengossa in the dark, advances on Wachau, which is evacuated by the French; Napoleon's men contain the Allies' advance out of the village with artillery fire, and Victor counter-attacks Wachau and regains it by 0930hrs.

2 0900hrs: Napoleon visits Murat's HQ at the Galgenberg and is briefed on the situation; he decides to send elements of the Young Guard under Mortier and Curial's 2nd Old Guard Infantry Division to support Liebertwolkwitz, and two Divisions of the Young Guard under Oudinot, along with a large cavalry force, move up behind Wachau in support. French artillery numbering 100 pieces and deployed on the high ground between Wachau and Liebertwolkwitz commences fire, which continues for roughly five hours.

3 0900hrs: Tsar Alexander arrives on the battlefield and observes the battle from the Wachtberg, between Güldengossa and Göhren; he is later joined by the Prussian and Austrian monarchs. Alexander decides to commit the Russian Lifeguard and Prussian Royal Guard, plus the grenadier regiments of Rayevsky's III Infantry Corps.

4 0930hrs: Kleist captures Markkleeburg from Poniatowski's VIII Corps; the village changes hands ten times by early afternoon.

5 1000hrs: Klenau commences his advance, quickly taking much of Liebertwolkwitz but losing it again just as rapidly.

6 1000hrs (approx.): Following an hour-long artillery and musketry duel, Allied forces storm Wachau but are unable to hold it in the face of a French counter-attack, which retakes the village by 1100hrs. The soldiers of Eugen's von Württemberg's 3rd and 4th Infantry Divisions suffer appallingly from French artillery fire.

7 1300hrs (approx.): Victor's II Corps attacks Wachau, supported by the 2nd Old Guard Infantry Division; the Allied defenders fall back.

8 1400hrs (approx.): Kleist's forces still hold much of Markkleeberg, but by this time all the other Allied forces have been driven back to their starting positions. Napoleon decides not to wait for Marmont and Ney, and has already despatched Bertrand to defend Lindenau; he launches a general advance by the Young Guard, Lauriston's V Corps, Victor's II Corps and the Old Guard.

9 1400hrs (approx.): Napoleon orders forward Murat's 8,000 to 10,000 cavalrymen, who penetrate the Allied lines as far as beyond Güldengossa, but as they are unsupported by infantry or artillery, they are consequently dispersed and driven back to their own lines.

10 Mid-afternoon: Dubreton's 4th Infantry Division leads Victor's II Corps into Güldengossa, only to be repulsed by the Prussian defenders.

11 1600hrs (approx.): The grenadier regiments of Rayevsky's III Infantry Corps and the Lifeguard regiments of Ermolov's V Infantry Corps are committed against Güldengossa, while Austrian grenadiers and cuirassiers advance on Auenhain. Some 80 guns of the Russian Guards Artillery deploy on the heights south of the village. Maison's 16th Infantry Division and Young Guard regiments counter-attack Güldengossa, running the gauntlet of Russian artillery fire, but are repulsed by elements of Udom's 2nd Lifeguard Infantry Division.

12 Late afternoon: Oudinot's I Young Guard Infantry Corps passes Wachau and captures Auenhain; elements of Mortier's II Young Guard Infantry Corps advance into the Universitätsholz, but are thrown out again by Klenau's Austrians.

13 1700hrs (approx.): The French mount another infantry attack on Güldengossa but are pushed back; Maison is almost captured. Following Allied cavalry attacks all along this front, the situation has turned to the Allies' advantage, with Napoleon's cavalry having been thrown back, his infantry advance halted, and his reserves fully committed.

Battlefield environment

The weather in the Leipzig area was cold, wet and foggy on 16 October 1813; it had been a very windy night, damaging roofs and uprooting trees. Recent heavy rain meant that the ground was muddy, impeding movement, and the fields around the various villages around Leipzig featured several ponds, dams, ditches, fences and other obstacles to hinder the advance of a formed body of soldiers.

The flat-topped hills south of Leipzig favoured Napoleon because they provided good artillery positions and masked his troop movements from the Allies. The Allied commanders

made surprisingly poor choices when deploying their troops, given that they must have known about the swampy and overgrown nature of the land between the Elster and Pleisse rivers, which would constrain their actions (Smith 2001: 72).

The villages were formidably strong defensive positions, offering excellent cover and fields of fire across the muddy stretches of land between them. Village houses were largely made of stone and surrounded by high stone walls, and the bridges over the River Pleisse south of Leipzig had been put out of action by the defenders.

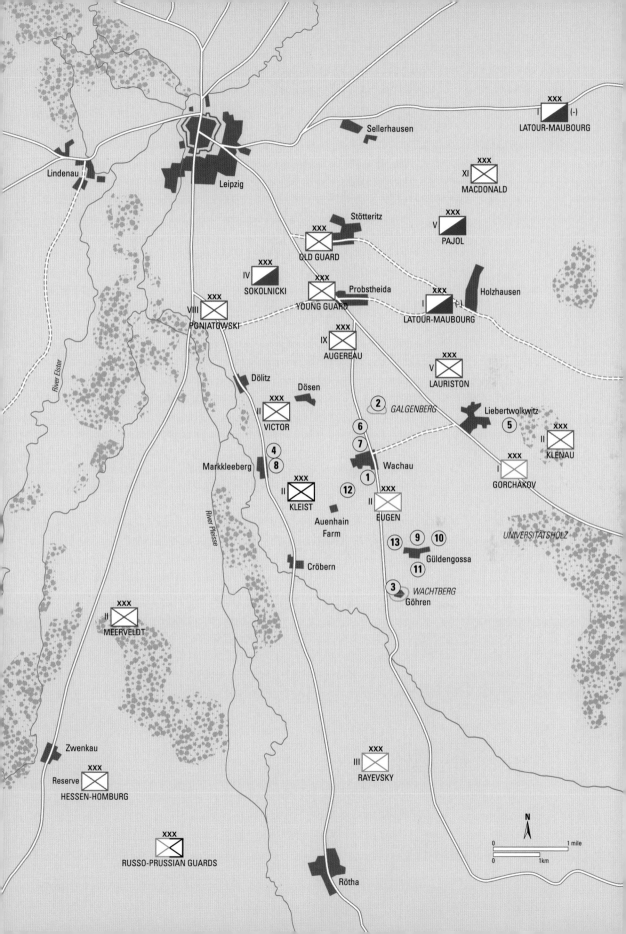

At this point it is worth pausing and building a more detailed picture of the nature of the fighting in Güldengossa, by consulting first-hand accounts of similar struggles being conducted elsewhere during the battle. The village of Schönefeld, north-east of Leipzig, witnessed similarly prolonged and bloody fighting on 18 October. According to one report:

> The flames which kept spreading through Schönefeld (nothing being done to halt them), combined with the tenacious defence, obliged the Russians to vacate the village a second time. Many wounded of both sides were burnt to death … Local people said that the noise and shouting of the troops, the sound of artillery and small-arms fire, the landing and explosion of shells, the howling, moaning and lowing of human beings and cattle, the whimpering and calls for help from the wounded and those who lay half-buried alive under masonry, blazing planks and beams was hideous. The smoke, dust and fumes made the day so dark that nobody could tell what time it was. (Quoted in Brett-James 1970: 178–79)

Conditions like these must have proved frightening and disorienting for both sides in the battle for Güldengossa; black-powder warfare generates substantial amounts of dirty-white smoke even in open countryside, and so visibility must have been poor, impeding command and control (Maughan 1999: 30). The very act of storming a village, whose narrow streets and passageways would play havoc with close-order formations, meant that even after a successful attack, the new occupiers risked being disordered and vulnerable if they were counter-attacked before consolidating their position. With respect to the struggle for Schönefeld, the Russian senior commander in that sector, General of Infantry Louis Langeron, later recalled:

> I believed the position was assured and went forward of the village to establish a chain of outposts. At this moment [Maréchal Michel] Ney [the senior French commander in that sector], who was near a mill on a hillock about five hundred yards behind the last houses in Schönefeld, launched against me so unexpected an attack, and so

Erstürmung der Schäferei Auenheim bei Leipzig durch die Grenadier-Bataillone Call und Fischer am 18. Oktober 1813, by Balthasar Wigand. This image, depicting events two days later, illustrates well the cross-fire that could be offered by the defenders of built-up areas, and the way that even broad avenues like the ones shown here severely constricted the close-order formations of the attackers. Note the Austrian *Sappeure* (infantry pioneers), wearing brown aprons over their greatcoats, wielding their axes against the large wooden door of the left-hand building; few infantrymen in the armies that contested the field at Leipzig carried such equipment, severely limiting their options in street-fighting scenarios. (Getty Images)

impetuous and well directed, that I was unable to withstand it. Five columns, advancing at the charge and with fixed bayonets, rushed at the village and at my troops who were still scattered and whom I was trying to re-form. They were overthrown and forced to retire in a hurry …

Fortunately I still had considerable reserves, and after letting the regiments which had been expelled from Schönefeld pass through the gaps between them, I soon did to the enemy what he had done to me, because my columns were in good order and his troops were by this time scattered … (Quoted in Brett-James 1970: 178)

The confused, piecemeal nature of street-fighting was not something that infantry were specifically trained for in the Napoleonic era, and the slow-firing, lengthy muskets that armed both sides must have been difficult to wield in the cramped confines of Güldengossa and other villages like it. Replenishing ammunition and water supplies would have proved very difficult, and like all black-powder weapons the muskets used by soldiers of both sides would have quickly fouled up with residue, making it harder to reload and increasing the risk of misfires (Maughan 1999: 27).

To return to the battle for Güldengossa: Maison counter-attacked and regained part of the town, before the Guards Jaeger Regiment was committed, and along with other regiments performed a bayonet charge to seize the town once more. This time, Napoleon ordered Oudinot's corps to support the 16th Infantry Division. The French advanced in three columns – Pacthod's 1st Young Guard Infantry Division probably on the right, with Decouz's 3rd Young Guard Infantry Division in the centre and Maison's 16th Infantry Division forming the third column, which was probably positioned to the left of the Young Guard formations – supported by artillery fire. Once more the French entered Güldengossa and again the town changed hands.

Things began to look bleak again for the Allies and some of the senior commanders began to consider ordering a retreat. Tsar Alexander had other ideas, however. After sending the Cossacks of the Lifeguard to help intercept the French cavalry, he rode up to the Finland Guards Regiment which, according to Lieutenant-Colonel Apollon Nikifoeovich Marin, was 'impatient, anticipating the minute of joining the battle' and shouted, 'Lads! To the fight! God be with you!' (quoted in Marin 1846 39). According to Pamfil Nazarov of the Finland Guards Regiment, the Tsar ordered the regiment 'to load our muskets and join the battle' (Nazarov 1874: 536). Now it was their turn, along with the Guards Life Grenadier Regiment, which had been incorporated into the Lifeguard in April 1813.

Major-General Karl Ivanovich Bistrom, now a brigade commander in the 2nd Lifeguard Infantry Division, commanded the Russian regiments that were to retake the town – a mixture of units

Tsar Alexander watches the Finland Guards Regiment advancing towards Güldengossa, 16 October 1813. A wounded officer (right), probably Major-General Kryzhanovsky, is being stretchered off the battlefield, while his regiment continues its advance. (From S. Gulevich's *Istoria Leib Gvardii Finlandskago Polka*)

from Choglokov's 1st Grenadier Division and the two Lifeguard Infantry Divisions. The plan was to launch a three-pronged attack. The Finland Guards Regiment was to attack the left side of the town, while the St Petersburg Grenadier Regiment closed in from the right. The Guards Life Grenadier Regiment and Guards Jaeger Regiment, plus the Tauride Grenadier Regiment, were to attack the centre.

The 1st and 2nd Battalions of the Finland Guards Regiment would advance towards the left edge of the town, while the 3rd Battalion, under the command of Colonel Alexander Karlovich Zherve, would make a circling movement and attack the sector closer to the middle of the town. The 1st and 3rd Battalions would simultaneously attack, while the 2nd Battalion, under Colonel Peter Sergeevich Ushakov, would remain in reserve. The battalions' advance would be preceded by skirmish chains, which would clear the way of any enemy skirmishers. Marin's history also mentions a Prussian volunteer battalion that accompanied the Finland Guards Regiment in the assault.

When the Finland Guards Regiment was ordered to advance, the soldiers gave a loud 'Ura!' and began moving forward in three battalion columns towards Güldengossa at a steady pace in order to maintain formation. They had not gone far when they were met by a hail of musket shot and cannonballs, succeeded by caseshot as the Russians drew nearer to the town. Pamfil Nazarov was one of those to be hit:

> I was wounded by a bullet in the right leg above the knee which injured the nerve and several shots passed through my greatcoat and my wound started to bleed, so warm, like warm water. And immediately I began to retreat, but a little way feeling the pain I fell face down on the ground and lay I do not remember how long. A wounded sergeant of our company approached me and recognising me began to lift me up. (Nazarov 1874: 536)

Soldiers of the Finland Guards Regiment climbing over the walls of Güldengossa. Note how the buildings are gutted and roofless; fire spread quickly in black-powder battle, even in sturdy stone-built villages such as those surrounding Leipzig. (From S. Gulevich's *Istoria Leib Gvardii Finlandskago Polka*)

However, with musket balls flying past them, the sergeant left Nazarov to find his own way to safety. Meanwhile the Finland Guards Regiment continued their advance upon Güldengossa, without firing a shot, but taking casualties all the way. Entire ranks fell 'but nothing was able to hold their steadfastness' (Gulevich 1906: 307). The 2nd Battalion stopped close to the town as planned while the 1st Battalion, under the command of Colonel Alexander Krestyanovich Shteven, continued its march on Güldengossa.

It is striking that the Finland Guards Regiment did not fire during the assault, but it should be borne in mind that it was well recognized at the time that once infantry began to fire, it was extremely difficult for the regimental officers to compel them to cease fire and resume the advance (Muir 2000: 79).

The first volley was carefully husbanded until the optimal moment, as it was likely to be much more effective than subsequent volleys. This was for a number of reasons – not least the progressive wear and tear on the muskets themselves, and the distracting influence of the noise and confusion of battle on the soldiers as they tried to reload (Muir 2000: 78). In fact, the decision to have the regiment load its muskets before setting off would have maximized the impact of that first precious volley, as the lengthy and complicated loading drill would have been much more successful in relatively calm conditions before the advance began.

Korennoi's exploits at Güldengossa, depicted in this 1846 painting by P.I. Babayev. According to tradition Napoleon is said to have ordered that word of Korennoi's feats should be published throughout the Grande Armée as an example of Russian bravery. This seems unlikely and no such proclamation has been found. Note the bare-footed prone figure in the foreground; even in the heat of battle, survivors appropriated the shoes and clothing of the dead or wounded to replace their own, meaning the fallen were quickly stripped of their possessions. (AM)

When the 3rd Battalion reached the outskirts of the town, Zherve and several of his officers climbed over a stone wall first, followed by some of their men. However, they were immediately surrounded by the enemy – likely to have been soldiers of Pacthod's 1st Young Guard Infantry Division – who began a fierce fire-fight and then as the French closed in on this band of Russians, hand-to-hand fighting broke out. A small group of soldiers of the Finland Guards Regiment, including Grenadier Leontii Korennoi of the 3rd Grenadier Company, helped Zherve and other officers get back over the wall, while another group held off the French. Slowly this small band of Russians were cut down one by one; Korennoi shouted, 'Do not give up lads!' Finally he was the last survivor and with a broken musket he continued to fight off the French as long as he could. With heaps of dead and wounded Frenchmen at his feet he, too, was overpowered.

By now the other battalions had arrived and engaged the other regiments of Pacthod's Division. Climbing over the dead and wounded from the previous attacks, the Finland Guards Regiment burst through the streets of Güldengossa and fought 'with incredible bravery'. The French were firing from every house, stone wall or other obstacle, and so had to be driven from these defences one by one. However, the Finland Guards Regiment was suffering heavy losses in the street fighting. Twice they had to fall back due to weight of French numbers, but on the third assault the Russians managed to seize their allotted sector of the town.

The other Russian regiments were also making good progress despite the fierce resistance they were encountering; finally the French were driven from the town and it was their turn to counter-attack. Again, the Young Guard

Mêlée in Güldengossa

Here we see the soldiers of Korennoi's 3rd Grenadier Company – distinguished by their moustaches, long shako-plumes and red-over-light-blue pompons – striving to protect their commander, Colonel Zherve (right), as he hurriedly withdraws. We have chosen to depict the Finland Guards Regiment in greatcoats and winter legwear; it is not clear when in the 1813 campaign the summer garb gave way to the winter equivalent.

The French attackers, *voltigeurs* of Pacthod's Division, also wear greatcoats; only the NCO at left retains the sabre.

The smoky, noisy battlefield must have proved a bewildering setting for the soldiers of both sides as they contested the stone buildings of Güldengossa and the other settlements to the south of Leipzig.

managed to gain a foothold in the town, only to lose it once more. It was probably this attack that Major Charles Pierre Lubin, Baron Griois of the Guard Foot Artillery, recalls:

> Towards evening, we took up a position more in the rear several hundred fathoms from where we continued our fire, principally directed on a town a little forward from our left, Gossa, I believe the enemy occupied. Several infantry attacks were made to seize [this town] but in vain. When night had almost fallen a final assault was vigorously executed and to the repeated shouts of 'Vive le Emperor!' against this town by two divisions of the Young Guard under the orders of General Curial [*sic*]. But he had no more success than the previous attacks. (Griois 1909: I.246)

The Young Guard were driven out of the town again with heavy losses. In his report Bistrom stated: 'Major-General Kryzhanovski, as is well known a brave general with his detachment, that is the Finlandski and St Petersburg Regiments, utterly drove the enemy out from the left side of the town' (Gulevich 1906: 308). The Tsar had witnessed the regiment's action and sent his brother the Grand Duke Constantine, always a stickler for military discipline, to congratulate the regiment in person, saying 'Thank you, Finlandski, the sovereign saw you and orders me to give his thanks'. To which the regiment shouted, 'Ura! Very good, sir!' All this time the sound of musket shots could still be heard (Marin 1846: 40).

Pamfil Nazarov, Finland Guards Regiment

In the ranks of the 6th Jaeger Company of the Finland Guards Regiment was a young recruit called Pamfil Nazarov. He had been among the reinforcements who joined the regiment in July 1813 in time to take part in the siege of Danzig. He watched as the elements of Schwarzenberg's army advanced, only to be pushed back towards Güldengossa.

Nazarov, who was wounded at the beginning of his regiment's assault on the town, would wander the lanes of Saxony for the next 13 days with other wounded comrades looking for treatment. It would not be until he reached Pleven that he finally found help. By then his leg had become badly infected. He records that the town was full of wounded and he was sent to a church that had been converted into a makeshift hospital housing 400 patients. For more than six weeks he remained there, while his leg slowly healed. When he finally recovered he found that his right leg was now 2cm shorter than the left one. Upon his discharge from hospital he had a relapse after only marching 6.5km, so that he had to be hospitalized again. He recovered, however, and witnessed the surrender of Paris in 1814.

Nicolas Marchal, 2nd Voltigeurs

In striking contrast to the young and inexperienced Nazarov, who was experiencing his first battle, the 2nd Voltigeurs' regimental commander, Nicolas Marchal, was a 43-year-old veteran who had been wounded as long ago as 1793 and had survived the rigours of the Russian campaign, despite being wounded at Borodino.

Like all regimental commanders, Marchal would probably have been mounted during the battle of Leipzig; this would have improved his view of events, but made him a more prominent target. Orders would have reached him via messenger, and he would have issued his own instructions verbally, employing his regimental staff officers to convey his orders.

Major Marchal had led the 2nd Voltigeurs for only a short time in mid-October 1813, having been transferred from the 93rd Regiment of the Line to replace Jean-Paul-Adam Schramm, the 2nd Voltigeurs' young commander in the earlier battles of the 1813 campaign, following the latter's promotion to Général de brigade. Marchal would survive the battle of Leipzig and take command of the reconstituted 7th Voltigeurs in the fateful 'Hundred Days' campaign of 1815.

By now it was night and the darkness put an end to the fighting. At the beginning of the battle the Finland Guards Regiment had mustered 48 officers, 140 NCOs, 43 musicians, 1,195 men and 83 non-combatants. However, despite attacking towards the end of the day it suffered four officers killed, four officers mortally wounded, 15 officers badly wounded, eight NCOs killed and 32 wounded, and 90 men killed, 292 wounded and 42 missing – a casualty rate of 52.1 per cent for the officers and 33.6 per cent for the other ranks. In all it had fired 60,200 cartridges, an average of about 50 shots per man (Rostkovski 1881: 197).

The commander of the Finland Guards Regiment, Major-General Kryzhanovsky, received four wounds while leading the regiment towards Güldengossa. Despite having been hit by three bullets in the legs, he did not abandon his post until he was struck in the chest, which caused a severe contusion. With his chest swelling, making it difficult to breathe, and blood flowing from his leg wounds he was finally forced to abandon the field. All three of the battalion commanders – Shteven, Zherve and Ushakov – were also wounded. Each would receive the Order of St George, the highest military award. Their citation read, 'being despatched to capture by assault the left flank of the town, with excellent courage and fearlessness attacked at the bayonet point and putting to flight superior forces of the enemy, [and] stubbornly defending the town' (Gulevich 1906: 311). Other officers gained lesser awards and some also received financial rewards, Kryzhanovsky being awarded 500 gold roubles and Shteven 300 gold roubles, while others received either 100, 60 or 50 gold roubles.

The lower ranks also benefited, receiving the Leipzig medal; the Emperor of Austria gave one gold and two silver medals with scarlet ribbons for the commander of the regiment to award to the three most deserving soldiers. Likewise the King of Prussia gave 12 silver medals. As a battle honour the regiment received two silver trumpets with the inscription, 'To the Finlandski Regiment of the Imperial Guard in reward of the distinguished valour, bravery and fearlessness shown in the battle of Leipzig, October 4, 1813', the Julian calendar observed by the Russians being 12 days behind the Gregorian calendar employed by the rest of Europe.

Among the regiment's wounded was Grenadier Leontii Korennoi, who had been in the regiment since its formation and had distinguished himself at Borodino, for which he received the St George's Cross. During the hand-to-hand fighting it is said that he received 18 bayonet wounds before being taken prisoner. However, according to Lieutenant Marin he 'was covered in wounds, but luckily all the wounds were not serious'. According to tradition Napoleon visited a makeshift hospital and hearing of his bravery he had Korennoi brought to him. 'For what battle did you get this cross?' Napoleon is alleged to have said, pointing towards his St George's Medal. 'For Borodino,' Korennoi replied. Napoleon patted him on the shoulder and ordered that he be released after the battle. A few days later Korennoi rejoined the men of his regiment, who were overjoyed to see 'Uncle Korennoi' again.

Owing to its losses, the Finland Guards Regiment would take no further part in the battle. Out of necessity the 2nd Voltigeurs, along with the other regiments of the Young Guard, would go on to fight and sustain heavy casualties on the 18th and 19th. Unfortunately, no such detailed data exists for the Young Guard at Leipzig, but the officer-casualty figures are known: the 2nd Voltigeurs had no officers killed, but one officer, a Capitaine Daviel, was wounded on the 16th; a further seven officers of the regiment would be wounded in the coming three days. On 1 August 1813, the two battalions of the 2nd Voltigeurs mustered 33 officers and 902 other ranks (Oliver & Partridge 2002: 17); by 1 November 1813, the regiment totalled just 25 officers and 281 other ranks.

As for the battle, for the Allies in the southern sector the Tsar had thrown in the reserves just at the right moment. The French cavalry had been forced to retreat, and with the Allied recapture of towns like Güldengossa Napoleon had failed in his aim of defeating Schwarzenberg's Army of Bohemia. Napoleon had also come very close to besting Blücher's Army of Silesia to the north of Leipzig, but he had to commit his reserves early in the battle so when the crisis came, he lacked the troops to inflict a decisive reverse on the Allies on 16 October. The Allies had lost about 38,000 men killed and wounded and 2,000 taken prisoner, whereas Napoleon's losses have been estimated at 23,000, with 2,500 captured. It had been the bloodiest day since Borodino, a record that would not be broken until World War I.

Even while the fighting had been raging, Allied units were force-marching towards the battlefield. The Crown Prince of Sweden, the former Maréchal Bernadotte, arrived the following day. Napoleon knew of these reinforcements; he also knew that to withdraw now might lead to the disintegration of his army. Therefore he decided to stand and fight on the 18th. In the mean time both sides licked their wounds on 17 October. Napoleon drew his battle line closer to Leipzig, so shortening the line of his weakened army. The clashes on 18 and 19 October were disastrous reverses for Napoleon, with the Saxons and Württembergers deserting to the Allies, and his decisive defeat at Leipzig all but put an end to Napoleon's domination of Germany.

Craonne

7 March 1814

BACKGROUND TO BATTLE

After defeat at Leipzig, Napoleon was forced to withdraw over the Rhine into France. He had been abandoned by his German allies; only Italy and the Duchy of Warsaw remained loyal to Napoleon. In November 1813, encouraged by the Crown Prince of Sweden's army in the vicinity, the Netherlands revolted against Napoleon's rule, forcing him to send the 12th and 13th Voltigeurs to Brussels and the 4th and 6th Young Guard Infantry Divisions to Antwerp to help put down the rebellion. However, he had transferred any Dutchmen within these units to other regiments. In November the Allies offered Napoleon terms, which he rejected because the proposed settlement would limit France to its 1792 borders. Although he still believed he could beat the Allies and bring them to terms, Napoleon did not have the luxury of an endless country to retreat into as the Russians had done two years before, which had so weakened the invading army. Instead, Napoleon had to rely on his military genius.

Allied forces approaching the Rhine on 1 January 1814, by Richard Knötel. The troops of Blücher's Army of Silesia, among them the men who would fight at Craonne, easily pushed aside the troops that guarded the French border. The invasion of France had begun in what some would call 'the campaign of the Guard' (Uffindell 2007: 104). (RC)

Campagne de France, 1814, by Jean-Louis-Ernest Meissonier. While locating his scene shortly after the French reverse at Laon in mid-March, Meissonier intended to convey a general sense of the gloom engulfing the emperor and his forces as the 1814 campaign wore on. Behind Napoleon are Ney (at left) and the emperor's chief-of-staff, Maréchal Berthier (centre). (© The Art Archive/Alamy)

Even before these negotiations of peace ended, on the night of 21/22 December Schwarzenberg's Army of Bohemia crossed the Rhine, followed by Blücher's Army of Silesia on 1 January. The Crown Prince's Army of the North invaded France from the Netherlands and in the south, the Duke of Wellington's army was also fighting its way across the Pyrenees. Alexander's aim was simple – the capture of Paris – and he would be the driving force in the forthcoming campaign, overriding his generals when they hesitated to pursue this objective.

Napoleon's aim, conversely, was to defeat each Allied army in turn. True, he did win battle after battle – Brienne (29 January), La Rothière (1 February), Champaubert (10 February), Montmirail (11 February), Château-Thierry (12 February), Vauchamps (14 February) and Montereau (18 February) – enabling Napoleon to parry each of the Allies' thrusts, but as soon as he defeated one army he had to turn and face another, allowing the defeated

Allied army time to recover. The Young Guard were always heavily involved in these battles, but even Napoleon's victories were grinding his army down further with losses he could not replace, and by March he was in a desperate situation. He tried to open peace negotiations with the Austrians, but this was rejected; all the time Alexander still pressed for Allied armies to march on Paris, rather than pursue Napoleon himself, forcing the French Emperor to react to the Allies' strategy.

On 27 February Blücher defeated Marshal Oudinot at the battle of Bar-sur-Aube. Napoleon advanced to meet this threat, but Blücher was able to withdraw over the Aisne and occupied the Chemin des Dames near the village of Craonne. On 6 March elements of a Russian corps group under Lieutenant-General Mikhail Semenovich Vorontsov clashed with Napoleon's forces near Craonne. During the night of 6/7 March snow began to fall as both sides settled down to sleep after what had already proved a hard day's fight, when according to the Russian general and historian Mikhailovsky-Danilevsky, 'two Russian brigades beat off two divisions of the French Guard' (Mikhailofsky-Danilefsky 1839: 220). After Ney's forces evacuated Heurtebise Farm during the night Vorontsov placed the 14th Jaeger Regiment in the farm as a garrison; a battery of 36 guns, deployed ahead of the farm, commanded the road approaching it from the east. The wooded terrain offered the attackers concealment.

About 1,300m behind Heurtebise Farm Vorontsov deployed the bulk of his infantry in three lines, roughly 500m behind each other. His cavalry, under the command of Major-General A.K. Benckendorff, consisted of the Pavlograd Hussars and four regiments of Cossacks, and was posted on his right flank. This was the only ground where the cavalry could manoeuvre. Several horse-artillery batteries were also deployed on the flanks. However, Vorontsov's command was just to be a holding force, which would keep Napoleon's attention while General of Cavalry Ferdinand Winzegorode with a large force of cavalry and infantry outflanked him and fell on Napoleon's rear.

Napoleon passed the night of 6/7 March in the nearby town of Corbeny, where he was visited by his old comrade, M. de Bussey. Bussey had often hunted on the Chemin des Dames and showed Napoleon various trackways that were unknown to the Russians. Having reconnoitred the position with M. de Bussey, Napoleon planned that Victor's II Young Guard Infantry Corps would attack up the slope and after capturing Heurtebise Farm would deploy in front of the Russian centre. Ney's I Young Guard Infantry Corps would attack the Russian left, south-west of the town of Ailles. On his left flank Napoleon placed Général de division Etienne-Marie Champion, comte Nansouty's

Michel Ney, *c.* 1808, by François-Pascal-Simon Gérard. Ney's impetuous and premature attack would severely compromise Napoleon's handling of the battle of Craonne. (RC)

Lieutenant-General Mikhail Semenovich Vorontsov (1772–1856). A soldier since childhood and a divisional commander by early 1812, Vorontsov was seriously wounded at Borodino; he fought at Leipzig and elsewhere before his epic confrontation with Napoleon at Craonne. He would continue to serve in the Russian Army after 1815, finally being promoted to field marshal shortly before his death. (AM)

MAP KEY

1 Night, 6/7 March: Vorontsov posts his advanced line in the wood and garrisons Heurtebise Farm.

2 0800hrs, 7 March: Napoleon rides up to the front line to assess the Russian positions.

3 0900hrs, 7 March: The French artillery begins to reach the plateau; it is approaching 1000hrs before it is deployed and ready to fire.

4 1000hrs, 7 March: Hearing the artillery fire, Ney's I Young Guard Infantry Corps deploys Pierre Boyer's 'Spanish Brigade' against Ailles, and Meunier's 1st Young Guard Infantry Division, supported by Curial's 2nd Young Guard Infantry Division, on the French left. The French succeed in pushing back the Russian skirmishers up the slope, but are counterattacked by the 2nd and 19th Jaeger regiments and recoil.

5 Late morning, 7 March: Ney's Divisions attempt a second assault. Boyer de Rébeval's 8th Young Guard Infantry Division, part of Victor's II Young Guard Infantry Corps, arrives and Napoleon orders it to march around the northern slopes to prolong the left flank of Ney's corps. As soon as he sees that Ney's skirmishers have gained the crest of the plateau, Napoleon orders Victor to attack with Boyer de Rébeval's Division, including the 14th Voltigeurs; the French succeed in capturing a Russian battery. A battalion of the 19th Jaeger Regiment and the Shirvan Infantry Regiment counter-attack the captured battery and retake it for the Russians.

6 Late morning, 7 March: Seeing that they are in danger of being cut off, the Russian garrison of Heurtebise Farm set fire to the buildings and retire.

7 Late morning, 7 March: Boyer de Rébeval's Division advances to the edge of the plateau under cover of smoke. Boyer de Rébeval's men, pinned by Russian artillery fire, are decimated.

8 Midday (approx.), 7 March: Sparre's dragoon brigade charges the Russian guns on the flank, capturing 12 pieces; two Russian infantry regiments counter-attack and drive the dragoons back. Sparre's men ensure Russian artillery fire before breaking and running in the face of a second attack by the two Russian infantry units. Seeing their flight, Boyer de Rébeval's men also break and flee.

9 Midday (approx.), 7 March: At the extreme right of the Russian line, French cavalry under Nansouty and Exelmans ascend the slopes in single file along steep paths; once they re-form at the top, they overthrow the Cossacks and part of the Pavlograd Hussar Regiment before driving two Russian battalions back almost to Paissy. A Russian reserve battery opens fire and checks the French; Russian artillery and cavalry then push back the French cavalry.

10 1300hrs, 7 March: Levesque de Laferrière's 1st Young Guard Cavalry Division, Charpentier's 8th Young Guard Infantry Division and the Imperial Guard reserve artillery arrive on the battlefield. At the same time, Napoleon arrives. The French reserve artillery passes through intervals in the French line and deploys in front of it, opening fire on the Russians.

11 1330hrs, 7 March: Blücher's order to retire on Laon reaches Osten-Sacken, who forwards it to Vorontsov; Vorontsov argues for staying put on the plateau, but Osten-Sacken insists that he withdraw and promises his 4,000 cavalry as a covering force.

12 1400hrs, 7 March: Vorontsov orders his infantry regiments to form square and they withdraw towards Cerny, covered by the Russian artillery.

13 Mid-afternoon, 7 March: Napoleon sees that the Russians are preparing to move off, and launches Nansouty's cavalry against the Russian squares.

14 1500hrs, 7 March: Christiani's 2nd Old Guard Infantry Division and Poret de Morvan's 9th Young Guard Infantry Division arrive on the battlefield.

15 Late afternoon, 7 March: Leading elements of Vorontsov's forces reach Cerny and he deploys 24 guns in line, checking the French pursuit. Vasilchikov's two cavalry Divisions repeatedly charge the French in order to save the Russian infantry and artillery. Osten-Sacken deploys artillery in two lines, which open fire alternately when the withdrawing Russian infantry reach the first line; the pursuing French infantry, in close order, suffer huge casualties during 20 minutes of artillery fire. Exhausted, the French cease their attacks; Vorontsov sends part of his command to Chevregny and the rest to Laon. The French do not pursue them.

Battlefield environment

At the battle of Craonne, the Russians had retreated to a well-chosen defensive location: 'Few positions are better adapted for defence than the elevated plateau behind Craone [sic]. On the left of it flows the Lette [River Ailette] between steep banks, and on the right are deep ravines; so that it is impossible to attack it, with a fair prospect of success, otherwise than in front' (Mikhailofsky-Danilefsky 1839: 221). Leading up to the plateau was a steep road. At the top of the slope, where the plateau was just 140m wide, was Heurtebise Farm, which with its high stone walls made an excellent defensive position. The French would have to capture this farm if they were to gain a foothold on the plateau.

This area, known as the 'Chemin des Dames', would be the scene of heavy fighting during World War I and the town of Craonne itself would be destroyed; it was later rebuilt further east from where it had stood during Napoleonic times.

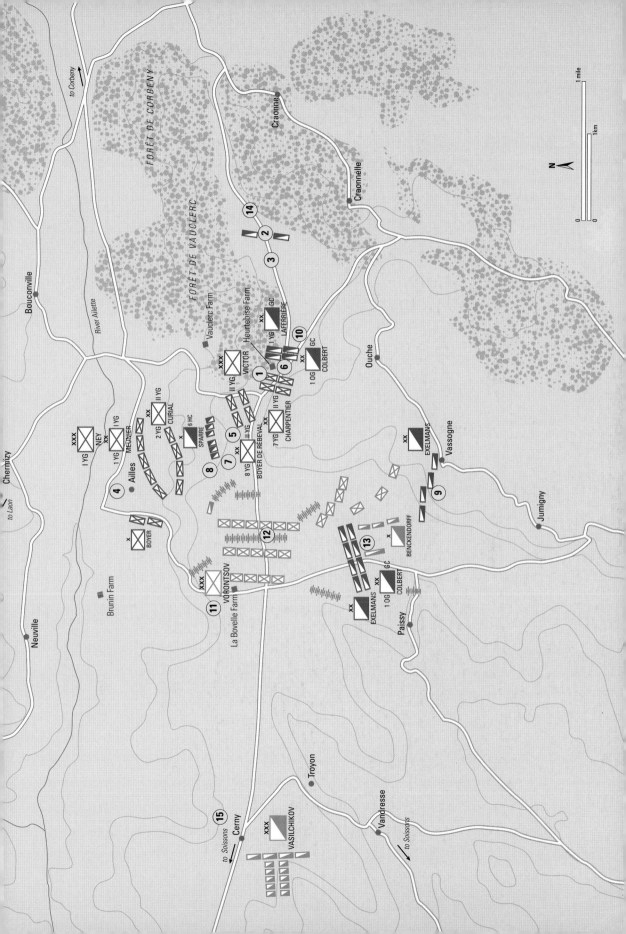

to Corbeny

FORÊT DE CORBENY

Craonne

Craonnelle

1 mile

1 km

N

FORÊT DE VAUCLERC

Bouconville

River Aillette

Vauclerc Farm

(14)

(2)

(3)

Heurtebise Farm

GC
xx
LAFERRIÈRE
I YG
VICTOR
(1)
(6)
xx
GC
1 OG
COLBERT
(10)

Ouche

XXX
II YG

II YG
CURIAL
xx
II YG

Chermizy

XXX
NEY
xx
MEUNIER
II YG

x
6 HC
SPARRE

CHARPENTIER
II YG

EXELMANS
xx

Vassogne

Jumigny

to Laon

1 YG
1 YG

2 YG

(4)

Ailles

(5)
III YG

BOYER DE RÉBEVAL
7 YG

(7)
(8)
8 YG

(9)

x
BOYER

(12)

(13)
x
BENCKENDORFF

VORONTSOV
XXX

(11)
La Bovelle Farm

Neuville

Brunin Farm

EXELMANS
xx
1 OG
GC
xx
COLBERT

Paissy

Troyon

(15)
Cerny

Vandresse

to Soissons

VASILCHIKOV
XXX

to Soissons

Imperial Guard cavalry and Général de division Rémy-Isidore-Joseph, comte
Exelmans' Line cavalry Division, which – once they had navigated the narrow
pathways – would encircle the Russians' right. The plan was that each of the
French pincer movements would attack simultaneously, but Ney's impetuous
decision to attack prematurely would have grave implications for the French as
the battle unfolded.

INTO COMBAT

The battle began shortly after 0900hrs on 7 March, when the French guns
opened fire. Rather than waiting for the order from Napoleon, Ney appears
to have seen this as the signal to advance. Général de division Pierre Boyer's
Spanish veterans of the Line were sent against Ailles, while Général de division
Claude-Marie, baron Meunier's 1st Young Guard Infantry Division advanced
on the French left, supported by Général de division Philibert, comte Curial's
2nd Young Guard Infantry Division. Screened by skirmishers, Ney's young
soldiers advanced uphill over rough terrain and in the teeth of musketry and
artillery fire; they succeeded in pushing the Russian skirmishers up the slope,
but were counter-attacked by the 2nd and 19th Jaeger regiments in a bayonet
charge and pushed back. These regiments had enjoyed distinguished careers
since being raised in 1796. Among the 2nd Jaeger Regiment's battle honours
were Friedland and Leipzig and those of the 19th Jaeger Regiment included
Smolensk, Borodino, Maloyaroslavets and Krasnyi.

Meanwhile, Victor's corps was arriving from the east and drew up to the
left of Ney's corps, with Général de division Joseph Boyer, baron de Rébeval's
8th Young Guard Infantry Division on one side and Général de division Henri
François Marie, comte Charpentier's 7th Young Guard Division on the other.

According to Chef de Battalion Boyer, Boyer de Rébeval's Division had only been formed during the middle of February from men who had been newly enlisted. The 1st Brigade was formed from three battalions of the 14th Voltigeurs, under Général de brigade Auguste Julien, baron Bigarré, plus a battalion of Flanquers-Chasseurs and a battalion of Fusiliers-Chasseurs. The 2nd Brigade, under Général de brigade Jacques Le Capitaine, was formed from three battalions of the 14th Tirailleurs and a battalion of the 13th Tirailleurs. According to the French historian Henry Lachouque, the Division mustered 63 officers and 1,582 men.

Despite only being raised on 11 January 1814 the 14th Voltigeurs had been formed from the remnants of the Voltigeurs of the Spanish Royal Guard, which had been disbanded on 25 November 1813, when Joseph Bonaparte, Napoleon's brother, had been deposed as king. However, despite having been part of the Spanish Royal Guard, the regiment does not seem to have been that well trained. Several accounts, including that of Boyer de Rébeval himself, record that the whole Division was poorly trained. Therefore the contingent from the Spanish Royal Guard may only have formed a small contingent of the 14th Voltigeurs.

Whatever the origins of the soldiers of the 14th Voltigeurs, what was going through their minds on the morning of 7 March? They must have known that some in their regiment would be killed, but probably believed it would not be them. With the sound of the guns ringing in their ears did they look to their officers and NCOs for reassurance, or did the more religious among them say a prayer for protection, as they looked up the steep slope towards the Russian positions? According to the former French civil servant and historian Baron Fain, 'the obstacles were diminished in our eyes by our eagerness to strike the last blow' (Fain 1823: 165), but many of those in the 14th Voltigeurs must have seen that it was a daunting task they were about to face.

After attempting a second assault, Ney's regiments managed to gain a foothold on the edge of the plateau, but again the French were forced to retreat. Being informed of this, Napoleon instructed Victor to attack. However, Boyer de Rébeval's Division was ordered to march around the heights of Craonne and support Ney's men. Orders rang out from the 14th Voltigeurs' officers and the drums began to beat the advance. Finally, Boyer de Rébeval was able to form his division between Victor's and Ney's forces and launched it into the attack.

Meanwhile, at the top of the hill the Russian artillery and infantry were waiting for them, including the 2nd and 19th Jaeger regiments. As the French continued their slow movement up the slope towards the plateau, their movement was partly hidden by a dip in the ground, but as they emerged began to fall, swept away by Russian roundshot. The burning buildings of Heurtebise Farm, fired by the Russian garrison before they evacuated it, also helped to screen the movement of Boyer de Rébeval's men.

Boyer de Rébeval's Division reached the top of the slope. The 14th Voltigeurs remained in column while the Flanquers-Chasseurs and Fusiliers-

Alexander Ivanovich Mikhailovsky-Danilevsky (1789–1848) began his military career as an adjutant to Kutuzov, in August 1812; he saw action at Borodino and was severely wounded at Tarutino that October. After Kutuzov's death he joined Tsar Alexander's entourage and was responsible for foreign correspondence and keeping a journal of operations. After the Napoleonic Wars Mikhailovsky-Danilevsky became a respected historian of Russia's involvement in the campaigns to defeat Napoleon, but always took care to refrain from criticizing Russian actions. (AM)

Chasseurs deployed in skirmish order. Le Capitaine's 2nd Brigade stood in reserve behind a small wood. So ill trained were Boyer de Rébeval's Division that he believed that if he ordered them to take shelter in the wood they would flee in disorder, so he had no choice but to keep them where they stood, exposed to the murderous Russian fire. According to Lachouque this bombardment lasted an hour, but according to Boyer de Rébeval it lasted for three, taking a heavy toll on the French infantry, but they continued to stand motionless; only the wounded left the ranks to seek help.

Vorontsov was preparing a counter-attack in order to drive Boyer de Rébeval's Division off the plateau. He selected the 2nd and 19th Jaeger regiments and the Pavlograd Hussars for this task. Orders came for them to shoulder arms and advance. Slowly the line moved forward, their straight, steady ranks showing that they had done this many times before. As the Russians advanced their artillery ceased firing so that they would not hit their own men.

The ceasing of the bombardment must have come as a relief to the recruits of the 14th Voltigeurs, but this was short lived because suddenly they saw the 19th Jaeger Regiment charge Boyer de Rébeval's Division, with their bayonets lowered, and shouting 'Ura!' That moment had come when a soldier must stand and fight or flee. Even the most hardened veteran rarely came to grips with the enemy, but now the 14th Voltigeurs began to waver along with the rest of Boyer de Rébeval's Division. A few men began to leave the ranks, but the trickle became a torrent, until the whole Division had given way, with the Jaeger close on their heels.

Mikhailovsky-Danilevsky describes this attack: 'Marshal Ney advanced by the ravine to turn our left wing. Here the Marshal made a great effort, but his column having been wasted by the fire of our artillery and charged at the point of the bayonet by the 2nd and 19th regiments of light infantry, the attack completely failed' (Mikhailofsky-Danilefsky 1839: 224). Fortunately for the 14th Voltigeurs and the rest of Boyer de Rébeval's Division, Drouot's Imperial Guard artillery and Général de brigade Louis Ernest Joseph Sparre's dragoons put a halt to the Russian pursuit and captured battery.

Seeing that the Russian horse-artillery battery had been captured, 'A battalion of the 19th light infantry and the regiment of Shirvan rushed forward with the bayonet and retook the horse artillery, which was for some minutes in the enemy's possession' (Mikhailofsky-Danilefsky 1839: 224–25). The 19th Jaeger Regiment, supported by the Schirvan Infantry Regiment, poured musket fire into the dragoons, before charging them with the bayonet, while the French horsemen were re-forming to take the Pavlograd Hussar Regiment in the flank. Under this musketry fire the dragoons broke and fled. The flight of the dragoons was too much for the remnants of Boyer de Rébeval's Division, and they continued their flight. The young men of Ney's corps also panicked at the sight of Sparre's dragoons fleeing in disorder and fled down the slope again, with Ney trying to rally them with blows from the flat of his sword and yelling at them to stop. They lost all their hard-won ground before they could be rallied.

By now Boyer de Rébeval's Division had all but ceased to exist and appears to have played no further part in the battle, having lost two-thirds of its strength. Meanwhile other French Divisions were gaining a foothold on the plateau, despite the efforts of the 14th Jaeger Regiment who held Heurtebise Farm. Finally after heavy fighting they were forced to abandon the farm, but not before setting fire to it in order to hinder the advancing French columns. 'Our troops successively ascended to the level, but the great difficulty was to establish themselves there. Marshal Ney and Marshal Victor fought at the head of the infantry' (Fain 1823: 168).

Just as his men reached the top of the hill, Victor was wounded in the thigh. He was forced to relinquish his command to Boyer de Rébeval. According to Lord Burghersh, a British soldier and diplomat, it was Charpentier who took over command of Victor's corps, but this may have been after Boyer de Rébeval had also been wounded.

Shortly after 1300hrs, Général de division Louis Marie, baron Levesque de Laferrière's newly arrived 1st Young Guard Cavalry Division also appeared on the plateau and charged the Russian infantry, including the 19th Jaeger Regiment who formed square, the traditional defence against cavalry. However Levesque de Laferrière's men were met by a withering fire from the Russian squares and artillery, which sent the French cavalry reeling backwards. The Young Guard cavalry rallied behind Charpentier's Division, which had by now moved up into line with Boyer de Rébeval's Division.

Also newly arrived, the reserve artillery of the Imperial Guard passed through gaps in the French infantry line and commenced fire. Further Russian attacks were made, but they failed to prevent the French finally establishing themselves on the plateau in strength. By now Nansouty's cavalry had also navigated the trackways on the Russian right and began to deploy on the plateau. With the entrance to the plateau secure, Napoleon was able to deploy his guns to full effect. They opened a murderous fire: 'The Russians being formed in three lines, within narrow bounds, sustained a heavy loss, whole ranks being mowed down, but the infantry never wavered' (Mikhailofsky-Danilefsky 1839: 223). Vorontsov was also able to bring his guns to bear on the French; he would later report that 'I had only to look on with admiration, and rejoice in the destruction which it [the Russian artillery] wrought among the enemy' (quoted in Mikhailofsky-Danilefsky 1839: 224). The first part of the battle had ended and now the French had to drive the Russians from the field. However, the French found that 'the difficulty of marching up the acclivity was extreme; the ground was contested foot by foot by the Russians, and it was impossible to accelerate their retreat by any movement on their flanks' (Fain 1823: 168).

All this time Winzegorode's flanking force was having difficulty marching along the muddy roads. With no hope of turning Napoleon's flank Winzegorode ordered his force to retrace its steps and rejoin Blücher's Army of Silesia. On hearing this news Blücher sent orders for Vorontsov to retreat. The order arrived at about 1400hrs, but Vorontsov decided to fight on since he was already heavily engaged.

Sergey Ivanovich Mayevsky (1779–1848) served as a courier in the Russian Army's main headquarters in the campaigns of 1813, seeing action at Lützen, Bautzen and Kulm; he was appointed *shef* of the 13th Jaeger Regiment shortly before the battle of Leipzig, and fought at Laon and Paris after his service at Craonne. His memoirs of campaign life in 1812–13, published 60 years later, are an important source of detail for historians of this period. (AM)

Again Blücher ordered Vorontsov to withdraw, but it was not until General of Infantry Fabian Vilgelmovich Osten-Sacken finally sent word that Winzegorode was unable to attack Napoleon as planned that orders were given to retreat. The exact movements of the 19th Jaeger Regiment are unknown at this time, but, according to Colonel Mayevsky of the 13th Jaeger Regiment:

At midday we were ordered to retreat … Unfortunately we did not have any cavalry, so the Count ordered the infantry to form squares (echelons). Wherever the greatest danger or the greatest fire was, there, of course, was Count Vorontsov. When he reached me at the very approach of the enemy cavalry, with amazing coolness he gave orders while we gloriously received the enemy and threw him back. After this we made a general retreat by echelons. (Mayevsky 1873: 271)

Mikhailovsky-Danilevsky places the time that the retreat began at 1400hrs, and continues:

Count Worontzoff, having made his regiments form in squares, ordered the retreat of the infantry to begin in ordinary time, and by alternate squares, and the artillery to follow. All the dismounted cannon, twenty-two in number, with the gun carriages, were carried off to the rear, as well as the wounded whom it was possible to remove. As soon as Napoleon perceived the retreat, his attacks became much more impetuous, and nearly overpowered the right flank; but Major-General Benkendorf, with the Hussars and Cossacks, attacked the French, and effectually

Craonne, 1814. This panoramic view gives a sense of the difficulties faced by large bodies of close-order troops moving across open ground. The neat formations seen here would quickly be hampered by uneven ground and numerous small obstacles, slowing and potentially disordering them in combat. (© Mary Evans Picture Library/Alamy)

checked them on that point. Seeing the extraordinary perseverance of the French, Count Worontzoff several times ordered the infantry to halt in order to repulse them, and then retreated as slowly as possible, showing that he was retiring not because he was obliged to do so by the enemy, but in obedience to orders. (Mikhailofsky-Danilefsky 1839: 225–26)

As the Russians withdrew, the arena of the plateau grew wider, which allowed the French cavalry to attempt to turn the Russian flanks. Fortunately, the newly arrived cavalrymen of Lieutenant-General Sergey Nikolaevich Lanskoy's 2nd Hussar Division and Major-General Sergey Nikolayevich Ushakov's 3rd Dragoon Division were able to counter this threat. The 6th Jaeger Regiment occupied a stone enclosure and also helped cover the retreat, firing a volley at close range into the French cavalry's ranks.

Osten-Sacken had also placed 36 artillery guns in a line with a second line, of 28 guns, to its rear. When the infantry passed these guns the first line fired canister into the French, and the second line roundshot and shell.

The carnage among the French was now horrible, yet they continued to advance in close columns along the narrow ridge. The thicker they pressed on, the greater the havoc; till at length the slaughter was such that their advance was impeded by vast heaps of the dead and dying. The French artillery several times ceased firing, but Napoleon kept constantly sending fresh troops to the attack; these, too, after sustaining immense loss were obliged to retire. (Mikhailofsky-Danilefsky 1839: 227–28)

This was probably the action Fain refers to when he wrote: 'The Russians were pursued as far as the high road from Soissons to Laon; the junction of the roads is called the Ange-Gardien from an inn which is there. The enemy made at that point a further resistance for some hours, in order to give the Prussians time to evacuate Soissons and effect a junction' (Fain 1823: 168).

So ended the battle of Craonne. All sides claimed it as a victory: Napoleon announced that he had driven the Russians from the field, while the Russians believed they had achieved 'One of the most renowned feats recorded in the annals of the Russian arms … In this battle there was hardly a regiment that did not distinguish itself'; however, he added, the battle 'was of as little advantage to Napoleon as to the allies' (Mikhailofsky-Danilefsky 1839: 228, 230 & 234).

According to Fain, 'Napoleon, after that sanguinary action, in all the dangers of which he had shared, still agitated by the uncertainty of battle, harassed with fatigue, and surrounded with wounded and dying men, found himself in one of those moments, in which the disgusting horrors of war would satiate the most martial disposition' (Fain 1823: 168). As the dead and wounded of Ney and Victor's corps lay on the battlefield, Napoleon wrote to his brother Joseph, 'The Old Guard alone stood firm – the rest melted like snow' (quoted in Headley 1993: 204). Napoleon admitted to a loss of just 600, adding the Russians had '3 or 4000 killed or wounded', and he had taken 2,000 prisoners and several guns. However, Fain recalled that, 'The only trophies left to us of the victory of Craonne, which was contested a considerable part of the day, were the enemy's dead' (Fain 1823: 168).

Recent estimates state that the Russians had 1,500 killed and 3,000 wounded whereas the French had 5,400 killed and wounded, including 1,645 men of Boyer de Rébeval's Division and 1,600 for Charpentier's Division. However if this is correct this just leaves 510 for Ney's corps, the Old Guard and the cavalry and artillerymen, who were also heavily engaged. Mikhailovsky-Danilevsky puts the figure at 8,000 French and 6,000 Russian casualties. The exact figure will probably never be known, but among the combatants it would be known as the bloodiest battle during the 1814 campaign so far.

Unfortunately, the casualties the 19th Jaeger Regiment suffered during the battle are not known, but must have been heavy. In 1816, in recognition of the regiment's bravery at Craonne, and at the battle of Laon a few days later, it was awarded two silver trumpets, with the inscription 'For bravery against the French at Craonne and Laon'. Boyer de Rébeval records that on the following day just 300–400 of his Division answered the roll call out of 1,000–1,200 men. The 14th Voltigeurs lost 30 of its 33 officers; other estimates put the loss of the rank and file at 70 per cent. The remnants of the regiment may have been at the battle of Laon a few days later and are said to have taken part in the battle of Fère-Champenoise on 25 March, before the unit was disbanded at the Restoration.

Analysis & Conclusion

After Craonne, the end was rapid. At the battles of Laon (9–10 March), Reims (13 March) and Arcis-sur-Aube (20–21 March) Napoleon was defeated and at Fère-Champenoise on 25 March the Allies overcame the combined forces of Maréchaux Mortier and Marmont. On 31 March Paris fell and on 6 April Napoleon abdicated; this was ratified by the Allies on 11 April, so ending the Napoleonic Wars – or so they believed.

THE RUSSIAN PERSPECTIVE

During the Napoleonic Wars the Russian Jaeger went from being near-automatons during the early years of Alexander's reign to being wily, experienced skirmishers capable of taking on the best the Grande Armée could throw at them. Their experience had been forged in battle; under the guidance of old soldiers the Jaeger passed it on to the regiment's new recruits.

The Russians siphoned off the tallest and fittest conscripts for the Imperial Guard and Grenadier regiments, of course, but between 1813 and 1814 Alexander ordered the raising of just eight new regiments; importantly, the modest increases to the numbers of the Lifeguard infantry, deployed in corps strength in 1813–14, were achieved by 'promoting' Line regiments, not forming new units. This meant that the vast majority of experienced NCOs remained with their own regiments and were

able to play an invaluable role in training and the preservation of *esprit de corps*. Even in 1811, when Alexander expanded the Line infantry and Jaeger arm, the 'new' regiments usually had a history as garrison or interior regiments and were accompanied by their own officers and NCOs.

At Krasnyi, after an impressive march to the battlefield the soldiers of the Guards Jaeger Regiment played a supporting role, befitting their customary open-order functions; at Leipzig, however, the Finland Guards Regiment demonstrated that despite being a light-infantry unit it could fulfil the shock, close-combat role expected of any infantry regiment, despite not having received any specialized training for the urban fighting in which it found itself. At Craonne, the veterans of the 19th Jaeger Regiment proved themselves the masters of every challenge thrown at them – even counter-charging enemy cavalry in order to recapture artillery pieces from the French. The Russian Jaeger would serve the tsars until 1833, when the Russian Army was reorganized; the Finland and Guards Jaeger regiments, however, would continue in service, and remained proud elements of the Lifeguard until 1917.

THE FRENCH PERSPECTIVE

Napoleon's Imperial Guard had been conceived as an elite combat reserve and while it remained a small, well-trained organization it fulfilled this role. However, once it was dramatically increased in size it was no longer the force it was originally designed to be. In 1813–14 Napoleon ordered the raising of a staggering 60 additional infantry regiments, 32 of which were Line units; in 1814, an additional 38 battalions were added to the establishment of the Young Guard, since each regiment had to raise a third battalion. Many of these newly raised regiments were understrength; moreover, by allocating the conscripts to these new units the military authorities found that the older regiments also fell below their paper establishments. These new regiments still needed their full complement of officers and NCOs, which had to be found either in the Imperial Guard itself or the Line regiments, which further undermined the fighting capabilities of the field armies.

In the three battles examined here, the strong *esprit de corps* of the Young Guard regiments was severely hampered. At Krasnyi the appalling weather conditions and lack of combined-arms support sealed the fate of the young soldiers of the 1st Voltigeurs and their comrades in the Tirailleurs and Flanquers. At Leipzig, the striking potential of the two Young Guard corps – potentially a decisive asset if employed en masse – was compromised by Napoleon's need to fight on two fronts on a battlefield dominated by difficult terrain and fortress-like villages that restricted the manoeuvres of troops on both sides. At Craonne the Young Guard's inexperience and lack of training, and Ney's impetuous decision to commit his troops too early, meant that the 14th Voltigeurs suffered appalling losses in a battle marked by its lack of tactical finesse on the French side.

Following the installation of King Louis XVIII, the Young Guard regiments were ordered to be disbanded along with the rest of Napoleon's Imperial Guard, as it was considered inappropriate that soldiers of such an organization should guard the king. The officers were put on half-pay, a military term for retirement, and the soldiers either discharged or transferred to the Line regiments. The Imperial Guard, including the Young Guard, would briefly be re-formed in 1815 when Napoleon returned, however, and several regiments would see action at Waterloo before the First Empire finally passed into history.

THE RECKONING

What of the fate of those private soldiers who served in the Young Guard or the Jaeger regiments of the Russian Army? Many, of course, survived wounds or sickness to take their place in civilian life after the wars – or to remain in the armed forces. After the surrender of Paris, Pamfil Nazarov continued to serve in the Army until 1836 and appears to have died a few years after completing his memoirs. Among the 872 wounded soldiers of the Russian Army who were lucky enough to receive a pension for their part in the 1812 campaign was Private Evdokim Ivanov of the 24th Jaeger Regiment, serving in the 5th Infantry Division, who received 25 roubles a year after his right arm was blown off at the battle of Klyastitsy on 31 July 1812. He was lucky, because others just received only 18 roubles a year. An examination of 200 of these pensions shows that 56 per cent received upper-limb wounds, and 26 per cent lower-limb wounds, whereas just 10.5 per cent received wounds to the body and 3 per cent had head wounds. The other 4.5 per cent sustained miscellaneous injuries or their wounds are not recorded. The low percentage of the body and head wounds would suggest that a soldier was less likely to survive if seriously wounded in these areas. These percentages would almost certainly be found in the French, as well as in other armies (*Russkii Invalid Supplement* 1815: 1–12).

Many, though, would have found a soldier's grave, like the one discovered in 2002 in Vilnius in Lithuania, where a pit containing 3,269 skeletons from Napoleon's army was discovered. They had suffered the rigours of the 1812 campaign, only to die at the very end. An examination of a sample of 430 male skeletons reveals that the youngest was about 15 and one was between 50 and 60 years old; the majority, 211, were in their early 20s, and 115 were in their late 20s. A Napoleonic soldier was far more likely to die of disease than in battle. During the winter of 1812 many soldiers died from hypothermia, but a study of 35 soldiers from the Vilnius grave reveals that ten suffered from typhus, which is highly contagious, being passed from person to person by lice. The majority of cases are to be found in 15 to 30-year-olds, the age range of many soldiers who served during the Napoleonic period. Among the Vilnius bones were fragments of uniforms; at least one of the buttons discovered was that of Napoleon's Imperial Guard, so in death despite all the privileges of the Guard its men were buried in the same grave as soldiers from the Line regiments.

UNIT ORGANIZATIONS

Russian Jaeger regiment

Similarly organized to Russia's infantry and grenadier regiments, each Jaeger regiment typically sent two battalions on campaign – with the exception of the Lifeguard regiments, which fielded three battalions each. Each battalion was divided into four companies, each comprising two platoons; one company was made up of the grenadier and marksman platoons.

Each Jaeger regiment had a *shef* (chief) who nominally headed the unit, but in the field a *polkovnik* (colonel) commanded it. Other regimental staff included one *podpolkovnik* (lieutenant-colonel) and one major; the *shef* was assisted by an *adjutant shefa* (chief's adjutant), while each of the battalion commanders was assisted by a *batalionnyi adjutant* (battalion adjutant). The staff also included a *kaznachei* (treasurer) and a *kvartirmeister* (quartermaster), both normally lieutenants, plus non-combatants such as musicians and craftsmen. Each company was typically led by a *kapitan* (captain) or *poruchik* (lieutenant), assisted by a *podporuchik* (sub-lieutenant) and a *praporshchik* (ensign); a *feldfebel* (senior NCO), 6–12 *unterofitsery* (junior NCOs), three drummers and about 140 enlisted men completed the company's notional strength, although this would be greatly depleted on campaign. The soldiers were divided into *artels* of eight to ten men; the members of these small groups were expected to support one another.

French Young Guard regiment

According to Haythornthwaite (1985: 8), the original Young Guard regiments formed in 1809 each had 12 companies in two battalions; later, these units were each reduced to eight companies in two battalions, with a ninth company, of *caporaux-voltigeurs* or *caporaux-tirailleurs*, added to each regiment in February 1811. (Napoleon's intention was that these ninth companies would collectively provide a cadre for replenishing the Line infantry; the Fusiliers-Grenadiers and Fusiliers-Chasseurs similarly formed four companies of *sergents-fusiliers*, one per battalion.)

In 1810–11 each unit's regimental staff included the *colonel-major*, two *chefs de bataillon*, one *capitaine-adjudant-major*, one *officeur-payeur* (a sous-lieutenant), one *sous-lieutenant-adjudant-major*, one *surgeon-major* and his assistant, four *adjudant-sous-officiers*, one *caporal-tambour* and one *armorier*. Each Young Guard company was comprised (in theory) of one *capitaine*, two *lieutenants*, two *sous-lieutenants*, one *sergent-major*, four *sergents*, one *fourrier*, eight *caporaux*, one *sapeur*, three *tambours* and 200 *voltigeurs* or *tirailleurs* – approximately one officer and one NCO (excluding *caporaux*) per 40 men. For comparison, from 1808 each Line company had one *capitaine*, one *lieutenant*, one *sous-lieutenant*, one *sergent-major*, four *sergents*, eight *caporaux*, one *caporal-fourrier*, two *tambours* and 121 *fusiliers*. As with the Young Guard, there was roughly one officer per 40 private soldiers, but Line units had a higher proportion of NCOs – one per 25 private soldiers. Of course, on campaign, these strengths would be much reduced.

ORDERS OF BATTLE

Krasnyi, 16 November 1812

French forces (Napoleon)
1st Guard Infantry Division (Général de division Delaborde): 4th Tirailleurs (Major Robert); 5th Tirailleurs (Colonel-major Hennequin); 6th Tirailleurs (Major Carré); 4th Voltigeurs (Colonel-major Nagle); 5th Voltigeurs (Colonel-major Sicard); 6th Voltigeurs (Colonel-major Rousseau).
2nd Guard Infantry Division (Général de division Roguet): Fusiliers-Chasseurs (Major Vrigny); Fusiliers-Grenadiers (Major-Colonel Bodelin); 1st Tirailleurs (Major Lenoir); 1st Voltigeurs (Major Mallet); Flanquers (Colonel Pompejac).
3rd Guard Infantry Division (Maréchal Lefebvre): 1st Grenadiers à pied (Colonel-major Michel); 2nd Grenadiers à pied (Major-colonel Harlet); 3rd Grenadiers à pied (Colonel-major Tindal); 1st Chasseurs à pied (Général de division Gros); 2nd Chasseurs à pied (Major Rosey).
Hessian Brigade (Prinz Emil von Hessen).
Imperial Guard Cavalry (Général de division Walther).

Russian forces (Field Marshal Kutuzov)
Corps group (General of Infantry M.A. Miloradovich): II Infantry Corps (Lieutenant-General Eugen von Württemberg); VII Infantry Corps (Lieutenant-General N.N. Rayevsky); I Cavalry Corps (Lieutenant-General F.P. Uvarov); II Cavalry Corps (Lieutenant-General F.K. Korf).
Corps (Lieutenant-General D.V. Golitsyn V): 3rd Infantry Division (Major-General I.L. Shakhovsky); 2nd Cuirassier Division (Major-General I.M. Duka).
Corps group (General of Cavalry A.P. Tormasov): V Infantry Corps (Lieutenant-General N.I. Lavrov); VI Infantry Corps (General of Infantry D.S. Dokhturov); VIII Infantry Corps (Lieutenant-General M.M. Borosdin).

Leipzig, 16 October 1813

French forces of the Young Guard (Napoleon)
I Young Guard Infantry Corps (Maréchal Oudinot): 1st Young Guard Infantry Division (Général de division Pacthod); 3rd Young Guard Infantry Division (Général de division Decouz).
II Young Guard Infantry Corps (Maréchal Mortier): 2nd Young Guard Infantry Division (Général de division Barrois); 4th Young Guard Infantry Division (Général de division Roguet).

Russian forces (Grand Duke Constantine)
III Infantry (Grenadier) Corps (Lieutenant-General N.N. Rayevsky): 1st Grenadier Division (Major-General P.N. Choglokov); 2nd Grenadier Division (Major-General A.A. Pisarev).

V Infantry (Lifeguard) Corps (Lieutenant-General A.P. Ermolov): 1st Lifeguard Infantry Division (Lieutenant-General G.V. Rosen); 2nd Lifeguard Infantry Division (Major-General I.F. Udom).

Craonne, 7 March 1814

French forces (Napoleon)
Old Guard (Maréchal Mortier): 1st Old Guard Infantry Division (Général de division Friant), 2nd Old Guard Infantry Division (Général de brigade Christiani). Attached: 9th Young Guard Infantry Division (Général de brigade Poret de Morvan).
I Young Guard Infantry Corps (Maréchal Ney): 1st Young Guard Infantry Division (Général de division Meunier), 2nd Young Guard Infantry Division (Général de division Curial), 'Spanish Brigade' (Général de division Pierre Boyer). Attached: 6th Heavy Cavalry Division (Général de division Roussel d'Hurbal).
II Young Guard Infantry Corps (Maréchal Victor): 7th Young Guard Infantry Division (Général de division Charpentier), 8th Young Guard Infantry Division (Général de division Boyer de Rébeval).
Guard Cavalry (Général de division Nansouty): 1st Old Guard Cavalry Division (Général de division Colbert), 1st Young Guard Cavalry Division (Général de division Levesque de Laferrière).
Reserve Cavalry Division (Général de division Exelmans).

Russian forces (Lieutenant-General M.S. Vorontsov)
Infantry Corps (Lieutenant-General M.S. Vorontsov): 12th Infantry Division (Major-General N.N. Khovansky), 14th Infantry Division (Major-General B.B Helfreich), 21st Infantry Division (Lieutenant-General V.D. Laptev), 24th Infantry Division (Major-General N.V. Vuich), Cavalry Brigade (Major-General A.K. Benckendorff).
Cavalry Corps (Lieutenant-General I.V. Vasilchikov): 2nd Hussar Division (Major-General S.N. Lanskoy), 3rd Dragoon Division (Major-General S.N. Ushakov).

SELECT BIBLIOGRAPHY

Archival sources

Edinburgh University Library, UK:
LHB/126/16 Admission Register Royal Infirmary.
The National Archives, UK:
FO 65/- Foreign Office papers of Russian Empire.
Service Historique de la Defence, France:
Journal historique de la Division de Rébeval, par le Chef de Bataillon Boyer faisant function de chef d'État, 1814.

Published sources

Anonymous (1812–15). *Russkii Invalid.*
Anonymous (1896). *Istoria Leib Gvardii Egerskago Polka 1796–1896.* St Petersburg.
Arnold, James R. (2004). 'A Reappraisal of Column Versus Line in the Peninsular War'. *The Journal of Military History*, Vol. 68, No. 2: 535–52.
Austin, Paul Britten (1993). *1812: The March on Moscow.* London: Greenhill Books.
Austin, Paul Britten (1996). *1812: The Great Retreat.* London: Greenhill Books.
Beskrovnogo, L.G. (1956). *Kutuzov, Sbornik Dokumentov.* 6 vols. Moscow.
Bogdanovicha, M. (1863). *Istoriya Voini 1814 goda Vo Frantsii.* St Petersburg.
Bourgogne, A.J.B.F., ed. Paul Cottin & Maurice Hénault (1979). *The Memoirs of Sergeant Bourgogne 1812–1813.* London: Arms & Armour Press.
Bourgoing, Paul de, baron (1864). *Souvenirs d'histoire contemporaine: Épisodes militaires et politiques.* Paris: Libraire de la Société des Gens de Lettres.
Bowden, Scott (1990). *Napoleon's Grande armée of 1813.* Chicago, IL: Emperor's Press.
Brett-James, Antony, ed. & trans. (1966). *1812: Eyewitness Accounts of Napoleon's Defeat in Russia.* London: Macmillan.
Brett-James, Antony, ed. & trans. (1970). *Europe Against Napoleon: The Leipzig Campaign, 1813, from Eyewitness Accounts.* London: Macmillan.
Cate, Curtis (2004). *Russia 1812: The Duel Between Napoleon and Alexander.* London: Pimlico.
Chłapowski, Dezydery (1908). *Memoires sur les guerres de Napoléon, 1806–1813.* Paris: Librairie Plon.
Davidov, Denis, tr. & ed. Gregory Troubetzkoy (1999). *In the Service of the Tsar against Napoleon: The Memoirs of Denis Davidov, 1806–1814.* London: Greenhill Books.

Dumonceau, François, comte (1958). *Mémoires du général comte François Dumonceau.* Brussels: Brépols.
Edwards, Peter (2008). *Albuera, Wellington's Fourth Peninsular Campaign, 1811.* Ramsbury: Crowood.
Elting, John R. (1988). *Swords Around a Throne: Napoleon's Grande Armée.* London: Weidenfeld & Nicolson.
Fain, Agathon Jean François, baron (1823). *The Manuscript of 1814: A History of Events Which Led to the Abdication of Napoleon.* London: Henry Colburn & Co.
Fallou, Louis (1901). *La Garde impériale (1804–1815).* Paris: La Giberne.
Griffith, Paddy (2007). *French Napoleonic Infantry Tactics 1792–1815.* Oxford: Osprey.
Griois, Charles Pierre Lubin (1909). *Mémoires de Général Griois 1792–1822.* Paris: Plon-Nourrit & Cie.
Gulevich, S. (1906). *Istoria Leib Gvardii Finlandskago Polka 1806–1906.* 2 vols. St Petersburg.
Haythornthwaite, Philip (1985). *Napoleon's Guard Infantry (2).* London: Osprey.
Haythornthwaite, Philip (1987). *The Russian Army of the Napoleonic Wars (1): Infantry, 1799–1814.* London: Osprey.
Haythornthwaite, Philip (2012). *Borodino 1812: Napoleon's Great Gamble.* Oxford: Osprey.
Headley, J.T. (1993). *The Imperial Guard of Napoleon.* Newcastle: Worley Publications.
Hofschröer, Peter (1993). *Leipzig 1813: The Battle of the Nations.* London: Osprey.
Hofschröer, Peter (2001). *Lützen & Bautzen 1813: The Turning Point.* Oxford: Osprey.
Houssaye, Henry, trans. R.S. McClintock (2009). *Napoleon and the Campaign of 1814.* London: Leonaur.
Jomini, Baron Antoine Henri de (1992). *The Art of War.* London: Greenhill Books.
Koch, Frédéric (1819). *Mémoires pour servir à l'histoire de la campagne de 1814.* Paris: Magimel, Anselin et Pochard.
Lachouque, Henry & Brown, Anne S.K. (1997). *The Anatomy of Glory: Napoleon and his Guard.* London: Greenhill Books.
Leggiere, Michael V. (2002). *Napoleon & Berlin: The Napoleonic Wars in Prussia, 1813.* Stroud: Tempus.
Lieven, Dominic (2009). *Russia against Napoleon.* Harmondsworth: Allen Lane.

Löwenstern, Eduard von, ed. Baron Georges Wrangell and tr. Victoria Joan Moessner & Stephen Summerfield (2010). *With Count Pahlen's Cavalry Against Napoleon: Memoirs of the Russian General Eduard von Lowenstein (1790–1837)* London: Ken Trotman Publishing.

Marin, A.N. (1846). *Kratkii Ocherk Istorii Leib-Gvardii Finlandskago Polka*. St Petersburg.

Martinien, A. (1909). *Tableaux par corps et par batailles des officers tués et blessés pendant les guerres de l'Empire, 1805–1815*. Paris: Henri Charles-Lavuazelle.

Maughan, Stephen E. (1999). *The Napoleonic Soldier*. Ramsbury: Crowood.

Mayevsky, S.I. (1873). 'Moi vek, ili istoriia generala Maevskago, 1779–1848'. *Russkaia Starina (Russian Antiquity)* 1873, 8: 268–73.

Mikaberidze, Alexander (2005). *The Russian Officer Corps in the Revolutionary and Napoleonic Wars, 1792–1815*. Stroud: Spellmount.

Mikaberidze, Alexander (2010). *The Battle of the Berezina: Napoleon's Great Escape*. Barnsley: Pen & Sword.

Mikhailofsky-Danilefsky, A. (1839). *History of the Campaign in France in the Year 1814*. London: Smith, Elder & Co.

Muir, Rory (2000). *Tactics and the Experience of Battle in the Age of Napoleon*. New Haven, CT & London: Yale University Press.

Nafziger, George (1996a). *Imperial Bayonets: Tactics of the Napoleonic Battery, Battalion, and Brigade as Found in Contemporary Regulations*. London: Greenhill Books.

Nafziger, George (1996b). *Napoleon at Leipzig: The Battle of Nations, 1813*. Chicago, IL: Emperor's Press.

Napoleon I, ed. Charles de la Roncière (1935). *Napoleon's Letters to Marie-Louise*. London: Hutchinson.

Nazarov, Pamfil (1874). 'Zapiski soldata Pamfilova Nazarova v inochestve mitrofana 1792–1839'. *Ruskaia Stariana*, 1874: 529–56.

Nosworthy, Brent (1995). *Battle Tactics of Napoleon and his Enemies*. London: Constable & Co.

Oliver, Michael & Partridge, Richard (2002). *Napoleonic Army Handbook: The French Army and Her Allies*. London: Constable & Co.

Phillip, M. Le Capitaine Toussaint (1845). *Coup d'oeil ser la campagne de Russie en 1812*. Toulouse: P. de Motauban.

Pigeard, Alain (1998). *Revue du Souvenir napoléonien*, 1998, 420: 3–20.

Piotrovsky, Mikhail et al. (2005). *The Russian Imperial Guard*. St Petersburg: Russian Style.

Raoult, Didier et al. (2006). 'Evidence for louse-transmitted diseases in soldiers of Napoleon's Grand Army in Vilnius'. *Journal of Infectious Diseases* 193(1): 112–30.

Roguet, François, comte (1862–65). *Mémoires militaires du lieutenant général comte Roguet*. 4 vols. Paris: Librairie Militaire.

Rostkovski, F. (1881). *Istorii Leib Gvardii Finlandskago Polka*. St Petersburg.

Saint-Hilaire, Émile (1854). *Historie anecdotique, Politique et Militaire de la Garde impériale*. Paris: Penaud.

Ségur, comte Philippe Paul de, tr. J. David Townsend (1959). *Napoleon's Russian Campaign*. London: Michael Joseph.

Signoli, Michel et al. (2004). 'Discovery of a mass grave of Napoleonic period in Lithuania (1812, Vilnius)'. *C.R. Palevol* 3: 219–27.

Smith, Digby (2001). *1813 Leipzig: Napoleon and the Battle of the Nations*. London: Greenhill.

Sokolev, Oleg (2003). *L'Armée de Napoleon*. Saint-Germain-en-Laye: Commios.

Spring, Laurence (2002). *Russian Grenadiers and Infantry 1799–1815*. Oxford: Osprey.

Spring, Laurence (2009). *1812: Russia's Patriotic War*. Stroud: Spellmount.

Spring, Laurence (2010). *Uniforms of the Russian Army, 1802–1815: Volume 1: Infantry*. Leigh-on-Sea: Partizan Press.

Stoker, Donald, Schneid, Frederick C. & Blanton, Harold D., eds (2009). *Conscription in Napoleonic Europe 1798–1815: A Revolution in Military Affairs*. London & New York, NY: Routledge.

Uffindell, Andrew (2007). *Napoleon's Immortals: The Imperial Guard and its Battles, 1804–1815*. Stroud: Spellmount.

Uffindell, Andrew (2009). *Napoleon 1814: The Defence of France*. Barnsley: Pen & Sword.

Vionnet, Louis Joseph (2012). *With Napoleon's Guard in Russia: The memoirs of Major Vionnet, 1812*. Barnsley: Pen & Sword.

Weil, Maurice-Henri (1891–96). *La campagne de 1814 après les documents des archives impériales et royales de la guerre à Vienne*. 4 vols. Paris: Librairie militaire de L. Baudoin.

Yermolov, Alexei, ed. & trans. Alexander Mikaberidze (2005). *The Czar's General: The Memoirs of a Russian General in the Napoleonic Wars*. Welwyn Garden City: Ravenhall Books.

Zamoyski, Adam (2005). *1812: Napoleon's Fatal March on Moscow*. London: Harper Perennial.

Zhmodikov, Alexander & Zhmodikov, Yurii (2003). *Tactics of the Russian Army in the Napoleonic Wars*. 2 vols. West Chester, OH: The Nafziger Collection.

INDEX

References to illustrations are shown in **bold**.